BYZANTIUM
An Illustrated History

0-0-4

1/23/08

ILLUSTRATED HISTORIES FROM HIPPOCRENE

The Arab World
Arizona
Byzantium
California
The Celtic World
China
Cracow
Egypt
England
France
Greece
India
Ireland
Israel
Italy
Japan
Korea
London
Mexico
Moscow
Paris
Poland
Poland in World War II
Romania
Russia
Sicily
Spain
Tikal
Vietnam
Wales

BYZANTIUM
AN ILLUSTRATED HISTORY

SEAN MCLACHLAN

HIPPOCRENE BOOKS, INC.
New York

ISBN 0-7818-1033-7

For information, address:
  Hippocrene Books, Inc.
  171 Madison Avenue
  New York, NY 10016

Book design and composition by Susan A. Ahlquist.

Cataloging-in-Publication data available from the Library of Congress.

Printed in the United States of America.

For Almudena

CONTENTS

I. THE EMPIRE TRANSFORMED (A.D. 284–330)   1

II. THE DISINTEGRATION OF THE WEST AND THE
      SALVATION OF THE EAST (330–476)   23

III. AN EMPIRE WON AND LOST (476–695)   49

IV. INSTABILITY AND INVASION (695–912)   75

V. VICTORY AND DISASTER (912–1071)   93

VI. THE EMPIRE BETRAYED (1071–1204)   109

VII. OCCUPATION AND DECLINE (1204–1448)   131

VIII. THE FALL AND AFTER (1448–53)   153

IX. DAILY LIFE   171
     The Imperial Family   171
     The Poor   172
     Farmers   175
     Women   178

Businessmen and Trade	182
The Clergy	189
Outsiders	196
The Military	198
X. A GAZETTEER OF BYZANTINE MONUMENTS	203
Greece	203
Israel	210
Italy	212
Jordan	216
Syria	217
Turkey	219
TIMELINE	225
LIST OF BYZANTINE EMPERORS	229
BIBLIOGRAPHY	239
ABOUT THE AUTHOR	243
INDEX	245

I.

THE EMPIRE TRANSFORMED

(A.D. 284–330)

⇒◆⇐

In the year A.D. 284, Diocletian, emperor of the Romans, surveyed the lands that were now his. The fight to get to where he was had been long, but that year he became master of a civilization that was at its largest extent in its thousand-year history. The empire ranged from Britain to Tunisia, from Spain to Palestine, and included all the lands that educated men considered civilized. It was the center of everything. It had the most powerful armies and the highest achievements in law and art. To the Romans it was an oasis of peace in a hostile and barbaric world.

Or so it once had been. Diocletian's reign (284–305) was preceded by a century of constant turmoil. Two great epidemics had ravaged the empire. The first was smallpox in A.D. 165, followed by what might have been measles in 251. The Romans had died by the thousands, perhaps millions. The urban areas of the Roman Empire had been hit much harder than the thinly populated barbarian lands across the Rhine, making the Germans, who were always dangerous enemies, even stronger. During the third century, a great Age of Migrations began. Germanic tribes such as the Alemanni and the Franks moved over the Rhine, while the Goths invaded across the Danube. They were joined by a dozen other peoples, the seeds of a new Europe: the ancestors of the French and the Germans, the Czechs and the Slovaks, the Belgians and the Dutch.

Roman aqueduct in Caesarea, modern Israel. The Romans built extensive infrastructure wherever they settled. Aqueducts such as this one brought water from
distant sources to supply the empire's thriving towns.

SOURCE: Israel Ministry of Tourism.

At the beginning of the Christian Era   3rd to 4th centuries A.D.

Nineteenth-century rendering of early Germanic tribespeople.

SOURCE: Historic Costume in Pictures, by Braun & Schneider (Dover Publications, Inc.,
1975).

Researchers can't agree on why these migrations happened at this particular time. There may have been population pressures or war to the east, or environmental factors such as drought. Whatever the reason, entire populations were on the move.

At first these attacks were mere raids, but as time passed they became full-scale invasions. In 260, the Franks marched all the way from the Rhine to Spain, sacking Roman towns and villages as they went. In 268, the Goths broke through the fortified border along the Danube and sacked Athens. Three years later the Alemanni and Juthungi penetrated Italy and threatened Rome itself.

Nor were the Germans the only threat. Across the Syrian Desert, the Sassanids of Persia had developed a sophisticated and powerful urban society. They ruled over the fertile farmlands of Mesopotamia, between the Tigris and Euphrates rivers in modern Iraq, and the vast plateau of what is now central Iran. This civilization combined the ancient learning and fabulous wealth of the world's oldest cities with the fierce fighting style of the Asian horsemen. It boasted an immense, well-trained army. That army was now taking advantage of Rome's turmoil and harassing the eastern frontier.

The common picture of the fall of the Roman Empire is that hordes of howling barbarians swept over the borders, overwhelming the imperial army and plunging Western Europe into the Dark Ages. This is, like most stereotypes, mostly wrong. By the end of the third century, the "barbarians" were becoming very Roman. Rich Germanic chieftains imported Roman wine and luxury goods and often sent their sons to be educated in Rome. The tribes were not raiding anymore, they were coming to settle the lands their raids had depopulated. The Alemanni chieftains living in their imitation Roman villas in the Black Forest east of the Rhine decided they would prefer the real thing, and led their people into the rich farmlands of Gaul, modern France.

Sometimes these migrants were absorbed by the Roman Empire to become buffer states or *auxilia*, "allied troops." At other times, as much due to Roman mismanagement rather than any warlike intentions by the Germans, the two sides would end up fighting. When tribes came to settle, they were assigned an official to oversee the distribution of food and land. These officials, taking advantage of a weakening and preoccupied central government in Rome, often abused the Germans or kept promised aid for themselves.

The constant warfare made it necessary for emperors to increase the size and influence of the frontier armies. These armies became so large that they began raising their own generals on the shield and wrapping these men in purple robes—the traditional manner of acclaiming a new emperor. Sometimes entire regions would break away, and for a time there would be two or even three Roman Empires. Emperors tried to buy the soldiers' loyalty by increasing their wages, but to do so they had to take in more taxes and debase the coinage, causing inflation that canceled out the pay raise. Then they would increase the pay again, causing a downward economic spiral that left an alienated army, an impoverished working class, and a bloody string of assassinated emperors.

The luster of the once-victorious Roman army was as tarnished as the copper coins the new emperors were trying to pass off as silver. In 251, the emperor Decius was killed in battle with the Goths near Abrittus in modern Bulgaria. While many emperors had met violent ends, especially in that turbulent century, none had ever died at the hands of a foreign enemy. It was a terrible blow to morale, but worse was to come.

Only nine years later, the emperor Valerian marched against the Sassanids to avenge their attack on the Roman province of Syria. His army was surrounded. Valerian went before the Persian emperor Shapur and tried to negotiate a truce. Instead, the Persians took him captive. He spent several long years as a prisoner at the Persian court, where Shapur liked to use him as a footstool when mounting his horse. When Valerian finally died, Shapur had him skinned and preserved his hide as a trophy to show off to foreign envoys.

Many of the troops in the demoralized and divided army weren't even Roman. The ranks were increasingly filled with the very barbarians the Romans were fighting. The reason for the change was simple—life in the Roman army was hard, brutal, and, in the third century, increasingly dangerous. Soldiers were nearly always paid late, and in order to survive often resorted to pillaging the very regions they were sworn to protect. Roman citizens were no longer willing to put up with these hardships, and the emperors found it expedient to hire the barbarians who were settling in Roman territory to fight other barbarians who also were trying to immigrate. Members of the same tribe often fought both for and against Rome in the same battle. At the Battle of Catalaunian Fields in A.D. 451, the Romans won a rare victory over the Huns, helped by a contingent of Hunnic mercenaries.

The power of the generals and the unruliness of their legions led to an almost constant state of civil war. In the ten years before Diocletian came to power there had been six emperors. All were assassinated, three of them in a single year.

At first it appeared that Diocletian's reign would be no different; he certainly gained the throne in the usual way. While he had been commander of the imperial bodyguard he was thought to have been responsible for the deaths of two different emperors.

Diocletian proved to be a more reliable leader than follower. He had a deep sense of loyalty to the empire. Its preservation was an obsession with him. One of his first acts as emperor was to issue legitimate coinage. For a long time, silver coins hadn't contained much silver, nor had gold coins looked even remotely golden. But there simply was not enough precious metal left in the treasury to issue a sufficient number of coins. Undaunted, he began taking taxes in kind, mostly in the form of grain and other foodstuffs, and using these goods to pay his army.

Diocletian spent most of his time in the eastern, more prosperous part of the empire, where he could gather more revenue for his ambitious building and military programs. He usually lived in a vast palace in Nicomedia, in Asia Minor, modern Turkey. Rome was still officially the capital, but the wealthy East was becoming more important.

Money wasn't his only problem. Christianity, once a little-known Oriental cult in the backward province of Palestine, had grown in popularity until churches could be found in every major city. Diocletian, a devout pagan, could look out of the windows at his palace in Nicomedia and see a Christian basilica. New religions were always welcome in the empire; during the third century many new faiths came out of the East, but Christians refused to believe in the other gods or to make sacrifices in honor of the emperor.

To the pagans, this refusal was narrow-minded fanaticism. There had always been many gods, and while it was perfectly all right to add another to the mix, to deny the divinity of all the others was foolish, dangerous, and, even worse to the Roman mind, against tradition. Persecutions swept the empire during the second and third centuries, but the Christians always seemed to find more converts. At first the Church attracted the poor and dispossessed, but by Diocletian's reign it also included the wealthy and powerful. Christians could be found at the highest levels of the bureaucracy and army. Some chroniclers say that even Diocletian's wife and daughter were converts.

The Christian community would suffer again under the new emperor. Diocletian ordered them to make sacrifices in his honor. The cult of the emperor had been a fixture in Roman life for many years, and to reject it was treasonous. Most gave in. Those who didn't were beaten or had their property confiscated. Hundreds were killed. Some Christians were even used as public entertainment; they were thrown to the lions in the arena. But Diocletian couldn't stop the rising popularity of the young religion.

People were losing faith in the old gods. While the rich once supported temples as an expression of status, now those with money led a more private, secular life. Instead of the huge sacrifices of the first and second centuries, the third saw a redirection of spare wealth into lavish palaces and personal statues. The nouveau riche who had made their fortunes through rising in the ranks of the army or the court would rather buy a statue from one of the new assembly-line workshops, where the marble body was already completed and only awaited a head carved in the likeness of the customer.

Romans who did embrace religion were looking for a faith that emphasized personal revelation. Eastern mystery religions became popular. Many were secret societies with only a chosen few allowed to partake of the ritual. The cult of Mithra was the most popular of these; it offered a series of rituals and initiation ceremonies that brought initiates through ever-higher levels of enlightenment. Hermeticism, a mystical philosophy that espoused personal connection

LEFT: *Carved bone showing a dancing maenad from the fourth or fifth century. The maenads were worshippers of Dionysius and known for their wild rites.*
SOURCE: Museum of Art and Archaeology, University of Missouri-Columbia.

RIGHT: *Carved bone depicting Victory holding a wreath from the fourth or fifth century. Images of this pagan goddess were commonly used to commemorate battles.*
SOURCE: Museum of Art and Archaeology, University of Missouri-Columbia.

Marble relief showing the deeds in the life of Mithras. This mystery religion was the main competitor to Christianity in the second and third centuries. The central panel shows Mithras slaying the bull, usually interpreted as showing his role in the creation of all living things, or of renewal at springtime. The smaller panels show various scenes from the god's life, such as his birth from solid rock. The curved panel above the god's head shows the signs of the zodiac. Astrology was an important aspect of many mystery religions, and was banned in the Christian era for this very reason.

SOURCE: *Textes et monuments figures relatifs aux mysteres de Mithra*, by Franz Cumont (H. Lamertin, 1899).

with the divine, was also widely practiced, but it required long periods of study and meditation that only the wealthy could afford. In contrast, Christianity was open to all. Its talk of salvation and of a single, unifying religious force was a welcome message in troubled times. On a more practical level, the Christians did not waste their money on sacrifices and statues like the pagans did. They invested their donations in the community. They distributed food in times of famine and helped bury the dead and rebuild cities after earthquakes or fires.

Like the Christians, Diocletian was looking for something to unify the empire. His fault lay in thinking that it was himself, that all his people needed to believe in was a strong ruler in this world, not promises of salvation in the next. Minority religions were always welcome in the empire as long as they understood that religion was to be firmly subservient to secular institutions. His persecution, like the previous ones, was not meant to destroy Christianity, but merely to force it to comply with Roman tradition. A real attempt to destroy the new faith would have been as disruptive as another civil war. Diocletian wanted complete control, not a world without Christians.

Another threat to Roman unity came from the nature of the empire itself. The western half, made up of Italy and the provinces that are now the lands of Spain, France, Britain, and North Africa, was becoming increasingly different from the East, made up of Greece, the Balkans, Egypt, Palestine, Syria, and Asia Minor (modern Turkey). While the main language in the West was Latin, most easterners spoke Greek. The cultural divide extended beyond language. The West was mostly rural and underpopulated, with the exception of a few large cities. The East had a greater number of small cities, meaning that while urban life was not as grandiose, more of the population had access to it. Education was more advanced in the East; most Roman literature of the third century was written in Greek.

The East also had the advantage of a more stable economy and a much quicker system of communication and transport—vital in a preindustrial, urban society. Most eastern cities were next to the sea, where goods could come in by boat. In the West, grain had to be hauled long distances overland, a slow and expensive undertaking.

Early mosaic from Antioch in the classical style.
SOURCE: Turkish Tourist Office.

Rome, though near a port, was far too populous to be manageable. The government supplied free grain to Rome's poor, partly to buy loyalty but also to avoid the violent and destructive riots that always came if the food wasn't doled out in time.

The new powerbrokers were mainly coming from the East. Diocletian grew up as a poor and nearly illiterate herdsman on the Dalmatian coast, modern Albania. He was one of a breed of self-made men who rose through the ranks of the army on the basis of ability, political acumen, and a good measure of ruthlessness. The old Italian aristocracy was becoming increasingly irrelevant. The Senate was nearly powerless, and the nobles had failed to find another power base. The emperors of the second century A.D. had been men from established families; in the third they were mostly generals. What the empire needed now were men of action, soldiers who could keep the barbarians at bay and quash internal strife. The educated, landed gentry were of an earlier, more stable age. Their discussions of ancient Greek philosophy and Roman law, their patronage of the arts and circus games—these seemed irrelevant indulgences in a more warlike century. As men of action took control, the senators retired to their rural estates, their votes no longer needed nor asked for by the new military emperors.

The relationship between the capital and the provinces was changing as well. During the prosperous first and second centuries A.D., regional centers grew in influence. Trier became an important military command post for troops along the Rhine. Nicomedia became the de facto capital in the East. A young man wishing to get an education or to rise in the ranks of the army or government no longer had to go to Rome. The city was still the center of much wealth and influence, but the worsening situation on the borders meant that emperors had to be constantly in the saddle, leading their armies on one campaign after another. During his twenty-year reign, Diocletian spent only a few months in Rome. The real seat of power was now wherever the emperor happened to be.

With the decentralization of government, rural landholders became more important, especially in the West. They increased their power over the poor families who worked their vast estates. They became intermediaries between the government and the common man, and were called "patrons." Patrons took care of their charges, protecting them from tax collectors and helping them out in lean years, but gained more and more control over their lives. These poor families were often in a great deal of debt to their patrons, and therefore were obliged to stay on the estates and work, rather than seeking better opportunities elsewhere. The poor of the West had not yet become medieval serfs, but they were on their way.

The concept of the patron found its highest expression in the imperial family itself. Paintings of the emperor and his wife and heirs hung in courthouses and private homes, and acted as witnesses to legal contracts and trials. They were the predecessors of Christian icons, but it would be another century before the images of the imperial family were replaced with Christ and the Virgin Mary.

Diocletian realized the external threats to the empire were too great for one man to handle. He decided to share power, and in 286 chose another Balkan soldier, Maximian, to rule for him in the West. Both men would be called *Augustus*, the traditional title of Roman emperors, but Diocletian, as Augustus of the East, would have final authority. Each half of the empire had two dangerous borders. In the West, the Rhine frontier was threatened by various Germanic tribes, and the Goths and Huns raided across the upper Danube. In the East, the same enemies attacked the lower Danube, and the Persians menaced the Syrian Desert.

In 293, Diocletian decided that each Augustus should have a Caesar to take over responsibility for one of the problem areas. Each Augustus would adopt his Caesar as son and heir. The system of four emperors was called the *tetrarchy*. Diocletian also decentralized the army, taking power away from provincial governors and giving it to a large number of regional commanders called *duces*, or "dukes." The military commanders, however, had to get their funding from the civilian officials. This command structure had the benefit of being more flexible in emergencies as well as lessening the chances of effective revolt.

Remarkably, this arrangement worked. Maximian and the two Caesars did their jobs and didn't cause trouble for Diocletian. There were successful campaigns against the Germans and the Sassanids, and the Romans enjoyed two decades of much-needed stability. In order to ensure that his system would last, Diocletian abdicated in 305. He made Maximian step down on the same day.

Diocletian left the empire divided between two Augusti, Constantius in the West and Galerius in the East. They were elevated on the same day in their capitals of Milan and Nicomedia. Rome was too far from the frontier to be a real capital anymore. Diocletian assigned each Augustus a Caesar as an assistant. Constantius was given Severus and Galerius was assigned Maximinus Daia. All, like Diocletian, were soldiers from the Balkans. While they shared his humble background, they sadly lacked his discipline. They were soon fighting for supremacy, and the next few years saw a bewildering array of alliances and betrayals. Maximian came out of retirement for a time to make his own bid for power, but Diocletian convinced him to step down again.

The only figure to show any sort of credibility during this time was Constantius, the Augustus of the West, who in 305 staved off an invasion by the Picts in northern Britain. He died in York the next year, and his troops immediately proclaimed his son Constantine as the new Augustus. They should have accepted the Caesar Severus as the rightful successor, but their personal loyalty to their commander made them choose Constantine.

Galerius, Augustus of the East, wasn't pleased. He had spent much of his career trying to depose Constantius and become sole emperor. He didn't have the military strength to defeat Constantine, especially since he was sparring with the other Roman rulers (and the barbarians, when he had the time) so he accepted Constantine, but only as a Caesar. He promoted Severus to Augustus of the West. Constantine bided his time.

He didn't have long to wait. Maxentius, son of the retired Maximian, declared himself Augustus in Italy. Severus tried to crush the revolt, but his army switched sides and he had to flee. Then Galerius invaded Italy. Once again, the soldiers switched sides and supported Maxentius. Shortly thereafter, Maxentius had to fight off a coup attempt by his own father. Maximian was having a very active retirement. Diocletian's arrangement of dividing the empire had apparently done nothing to avert chaos and civil war.

At this point Diocletian returned. The aged former emperor enjoyed vast popularity with the people and military, and he was able to order Maximian to give up his title a third time. He appointed another officer, Licinius, to be the Augustus of the West. He kept Constantine as Caesar.

These directives didn't stop the fighting. Maxentius was still in control of Italy and Africa, the two most important provinces in the West, and all the other tetrarchs had ambitions of their own. Maximian came back on the scene but was quickly defeated by Constantine. The old Augustus then hanged himself.

While Constantine and Maxentius glowered at each other over the Alps, things were going equally poorly in the East. The borders were as insecure as ever. To shift public attention away from external problems, Galerius and his Caesar, Maximinus Daia, persecuted the

Christians. In 310, Maximinus Daia began calling himself Augustus of the East as Galerius succumbed to a terrible case of bowel cancer. Christian writers lost no time in ascribing his disease to the anger of God and took great pleasure in detailing his suffering. Eusebius, in his *History of the Church*, recounts the unpopular ruler's last days in loving detail.

"Inflammation broke out round the middle of his genitals, then a deep-seated fistular ulcer: these ate their way incurably into his inmost bowels. From them came a teeming indescribable mass of worms, and a sickening smell was given off; for the whole of his hulking body, thanks to overeating, had been transformed into a huge lump of flabby fat, which then decomposed and presented those who came near with a revolting and horrifying sight."[1]

In 312, Constantine finally decided to take over the entire empire. He crossed the Alps and defeated Maxentius' armies in two hard-fought battles. Soon Constantine was approaching Rome. Maxentius was waiting for him near the Milvian Bridge over the Tiber River, the last natural barrier guarding the city. Just before the battle, Constantine had a vision that would change history. He saw a cross of light above the setting sun, and the words "Conquer by This." He ordered a cross to be added to the traditional battle standard and promised to follow the Christian God if he won. Then he led his troops into battle and decisively routed Maxentius.

Maxentius had foreseen that things might go badly for him, so he set a trap for Constantine. Next to the narrow Milvian Bridge he had built a broad pontoon bridge to bring his troops across the river. He fashioned a key joint that could be removed to make the pontoon bridge fall apart. Once again, fortune favored Constantine. The engineers manning the bridge, seeing Maxentius retreating with Constantine's army in pursuit, pulled out the joint before Maxentius and his army had time to get across. Maxentius was cut off. He and his

1. Eusebius, *History of the Church*, VIII.16. Reproduced by permission of Penguin Books, Ltd.

troops crowded onto the Milvian Bridge, which wasn't designed to hold so much weight. The bridge collapsed. Maxentius and many of his soldiers plummeted into the water and drowned.

So Constantine won the battle and endorsed Christianity. He met with Licinius, the other Augustus, in Milan in January 313 and they declared Christianity to be a fully legal religion. Licinius then marched against Maximinus Daia, defeated him, and slaughtered his family. He took control of the East and let Constantine rule in the West. With the deaths of Maxentius and Maximinus Daia, there were now only two men calling themselves Augustus, instead of four. It looked like the empire might be headed towards another period of stability.

The acceptance of the Christian faith as the favored religion of the Roman Empire was one of the great about-faces of history. A sect that once was outcast from society became the very rock on which that society was based. Choosing Christianity as the heir to a thousand years of tradition was a tremendous act of faith. This faith was not in the Christian God, but the faith that the Church could take over the spiritual leadership granted to the pagan temples since the time of the early Republic.

Constantine made a wise choice. Christianity proved to be the only religion that could mobilize large numbers of people in every city in the empire. It had an active and dedicated membership that was loyal to the Church hierarchy and willing at the same time to be Roman. The Christians of the third century A.D. were not as alienated from society as either the pagan or Christian writers would have us believe. Many were leading citizens who respected the classical culture enough to commission works such as the Esquiline Treasure, a silver dowry set that displayed the name of Christ next to scenes of Aphrodite emerging from the waves on a seashell.

Once Constantine established control of Rome, he set about transforming it into a Christian city. He built several churches, including the original basilica of St. Peter's on Vatican Hill, and gave the pope a palace. The leader of the once-outlawed religion was now receiving imperial subsidies. Constantine gave the Church land and tax shelters. He proved vastly popular with the Christians, who still remembered the pogroms under the emperor Decius, when from 249 to 251 thousands were slaughtered in the streets of the city; not even the pope had been spared.

Licinius was less popular. While he nominally embraced the new religion, he was not nearly as enthusiastic as Constantine was. He supported pagan writers and gave the best positions in his court and army to worshipers of the old gods. He began to believe that Christians in his government were spies for Constantine. Soon Licinius brought back the persecutions. This blatant act was just the excuse Constantine needed to attack. In 323, he marched east. After the bloody battle of Chrysopolis on the Asian side of the Bosphorus in 324, Licinius surrendered on the condition that he would be given clemency. Constantine executed him anyway.

In the writings of Christian authors such as Eusebius, Constantine became a great Christian hero, while Licinius was turned into a villain. In the black-and-white of Christian thought they had to be one or the other. The reality was not so clear-cut. Constantine was not yet completely Christian. His mother had been one, but his father had worshiped the Sun god—Sol Invictus. Constantine claimed to have had a vision of Sol Invictus earlier in his life. Even his famous vision before the Battle of Milvian Bridge was ambiguous—it included a sun as well as a cross. It is probable that he never saw the vision. He didn't report it until much later. Although he claims his entire army saw it, the only record of it is Constantine's own testimony. Ever more telling is the fact that until 320, his coins bore a solar disc, with the inscription *Sol Invictus,* "the unconquered Sun."

Rendering of an early coin issue of the reign of Constantine. Despite making Christianity the dominant religion in the empire, Constantine often used pagan imagery in his coinage. Here the emperor is shown being crowned by Sol Invictus, the unconquered Sun.

SOURCE: *Studies in East Christian and Roman Art,* by Walter Dennison, Charles Freer, and Charles Morey. University of Michigan Studies Humanistic Series, vol. 12 (Macmillan, 1918).

Many of Constantine's decrees, while superficially Christian, were acceptable to both faiths. He banned gladiatorial shows and ritual prostitution, which were deplored as immoral by many pagans as well as Christians. He also established Sunday as a day of rest, but Sunday was just as sacred to the followers of Sol Invictus as to those of Christ. The day was even acceptable to the followers of Mithra, who considered their god an aspect of the Sun. It seems Constantine was trying to make monotheism palatable to pagans, while trying to get Christians to accept a more monotheistic paganism.

But problems came from an unexpected quarter. Christianity, which was supposed to bring unity to the empire, was going through its first major schism. In the 320s, an Egyptian priest named Arius espoused a controversial idea on the nature of Christ. Arius believed that Jesus was the Son of God, but separate from Him. While a perfect human, Jesus was not part of the Father or the Holy Spirit and was therefore an instrument of God, not God Himself. This concept was called "Arianism," and it sounded logical to many people. The idea that a god could be one and three at the same time, as the doctrine of the Trinity holds, made no intuitive sense. In the old pagan tradition, however, many gods had mortal sons, and they often acted as their father's agents on earth.

To traditional Christians, this idea was anathema. To consider Christ as separate and less divine than God would create a Christian polytheism and put Christ's position as the savior of mankind seriously in doubt. This tenet would undermine all Christianity stood for. The archbishop of Alexandria tried to get Arius banned from the Church, but support for him only grew. Learned men in the East followed the Greek model of education, which encouraged independent thinking, even in matters of theology. What may seem to the modern mind to be minor points of doctrine were of the greatest importance to them.

Constantine was not amused. He was a soldier, striving to create a secure base from which to fight the Goths and the Persians, and he did not want a bunch of overly philosophical easterners tearing apart what he had worked so hard to build. He fired off a letter to his subjects, stating the whole thing was "extremely trivial and quite unworthy of so much controversy."[2]

When that didn't solve the dispute, he called a council at Nicaea, in Asia Minor. Bishops from all across the Roman world gathered in 325 for what was the largest gathering of the clergy in the three-hundred-year history of the Church. This first attempt to bring together all the Church leaders for a single meeting set a precedent for centuries to come. Constantine convinced the clergy to compromise. Christ and the Father, it was decreed, were "of like substance," a statement vague enough to be acceptable to both sides. Arius and a few staunch followers didn't sign the agreement and were banished. Arius' writings were burned. Unity, it was supposed, had been restored.

The fact that the council was held in Asia Minor and not Rome showed how irrelevant that city had become. It would become even more so. Constantine began construction of a new capital at Byzantium, a small town on a promontory just across the narrow waters of the Bosphorus from Asia Minor. This location was ideal. It lay at the meeting of Asia and Europe. The Golden Horn, Byzantium's large, sheltered port, controlled the trade between the Black Sea and the Mediterranean, and was the outlet for the Silk Route. The city was surrounded on three sides by water, so it only needed strong fortifications on the landward side.

Constantine ransacked a dozen other cities of their artistic treasures to decorate his new capital and sent his mother Helena off to the Holy Land to find relics to put in its churches. She didn't disappoint him. When she got to Jerusalem, she dug around Golgotha, the traditional spot of the Crucifixion, and promptly found the True Cross. In the modern age she would become the patron saint of archaeologists.

The new city was built on a grand scale. At its center stood a four-sided arch on which Constantine put the True Cross. This arch became the zero point for all imperial measurements. A milepost in Greece that said, for example, "200 miles," meant that it was two

---

2. Eusebius, *Life of Constantine,* II.68. Used by permission of Oxford University Press.

Entrance to the Church of the Holy Sepulchre, Jerusalem. This church was originally founded by Constantine on the purported site of the Crucifixion and burial of Christ. It was rebuilt during the Crusades.

hundred miles from the Cross. From now on all Romans would know exactly how close they were to God. All roads no longer led to Rome, but to the center of Constantine's new capital. Constantine also built an immense Hippodrome for chariot races, where a set of stairs led from the box seating for the imperial family to an immense palace. Nearby was a hundred-foot column of porphyry, a prized purple marble. The column contained numerous artifacts, including the hatchet that Noah used to build the Ark. At its top stood a statue of Constantine. Its body was originally part of a statue of Apollo, but the head had been removed and a new one in the image of the emperor was put in its place. In one hand the statue held an orb with a fragment of the True Cross.

Throughout the city were broad streets, elegant palaces for the courtiers, and statues and carvings from across the Roman world. Constantine's capital was nominally a Christian city, but most of its artwork was pagan. The pagan historian Zosimus wrote that Constantine even founded two pagan temples in his new city, probably to Sol Invictus.

In 330, he renamed the city Constantinople, in honor of himself. While historians have generally referred to the eastern Roman empire as "Byzantium," after the city Constantine chose as his capital, the Byzantines themselves never did. In their mind they were Romans, and their capital, Constantinople, was the New Rome. It would be the center of the Roman Empire for more than a thousand years.

The Hippodrome at Constantinople. It is now a city park, but it retains its shape and features an Egyptian obelisk that Theodosius I (379–95) imported and erected on the Spina, a platform that ran down the center of the racetrack. Chariots would race around the Spina seven times. To the left is another obelisk, built in imitation of the ancient Egyptian one and erected by Constantine VII (913–59).

SOURCE: School of Architecture, College of Architecture, Planning, and Landscape Architecture, University of Arizona.

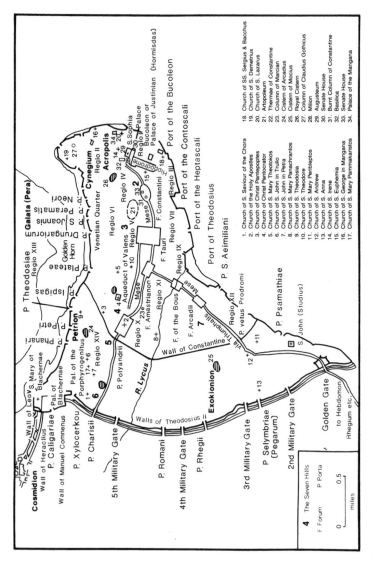

Map of Constantinople, showing the known monuments, public buildings and palaces.

SOURCE: *Cambridge Medieval History*, vol. 4, edited by J. B. Bury (Cambridge University Press, 1927).

1. Church of S. Saviour of the Chora
2. Church of the Holy Apostles
3. Church of Christ Pantepoptes
4. Church of Christ Pantocrator
5. Church of S. Mary Theotokos
6. Church of S. John in Trullo
7. Church of S. John in Petra
8. Church of S. Mary Panachrantos
9. Church of S. Theodosia
10. Church of S. Theodore
11. Church of S. Mary Peribleptos
12. Church of S. Andrew
13. Church of S. Anna
14. Church of S. Irene
15. Church of S. Euphemia
16. Church of S. George in Mangana
17. Church of S. Mary Pammakaristos
18. Church of SS. Sergius & Bacchus
19. Church of S. Demetrius
20. Church of S. Lazarus
21. Artopoleum
22. Thermae of Constantine
23. Column of Marcian
24. Cistern of Arcadius
25. Cistern of Mocius
26. Royal Cistern
27. Column of Claudius Gothicus
28. Milion
29. Augusteum
30. Senate House
31. Burnt Column of Constantine
32. Basilica
33. Senate House
34. Palace of the Mangana

II.

THE DISINTEGRATION OF THE WEST AND THE SALVATION OF THE EAST

(330–476)

———=▶◆◀=———

By A.D. 337, Constantine was an old and dying man, but he ruled an empire that was the most stable it had been since the days of Diocletian. He had defeated the Germanic tribes in a series of brilliant campaigns, and established an impressive capital filled with richly decorated churches and public buildings.

Despite using Christianity to unify his demoralized people, Constantine did not become a Christian until he was on his deathbed. Then he called for his bishop and biographer Eusebius, an Arian, to baptize him. The Council of Nicaea had not solved the Arian controversy. Constantine had eventually pardoned Arius, and Eusebius was one of Constantine's trusted advisors. Even on his deathbed Constantine tried to foster religious tolerance and compromise.

Deathbed baptisms were a common practice in the early centuries of Christianity. Baptism cleansed a person of all sin, so putting it off until the last moment when there wouldn't be a chance to sin again was always safer. In this case, Constantine got his wish. A few days after he became a Christian he died. He was laid to rest in the Church of the Holy Apostles in Constantinople. His golden coffin was placed inside a massive porphyry sarcophagus surrounded by twelve identical ones, one for each of the Apostles. The first Christian emperor had a burial ceremony that gave him the same symbolic status as Jesus.

Constantine left the empire to his three sons, whom he arrogantly and rather confusingly named Constantine II, Constans, and Constantius II. They inherited the empire and ruled as separate monarchs, each with his own army and bureaucracy. Inevitably, they fell to fighting. By 350, only Constantius II was still alive. He ruled until 361, but after he took power from his brothers he still continued the tradition of divided rule, making his half-cousin Julian the Caesar of the West. He also continued his father's building campaign in Constantinople, although a costly but victorious war with the Persians limited progress somewhat. The fight was over the status of Armenia, an ancient kingdom that had the misfortune of bordering both empires. Both the Persians and the Romans set up puppet dynasties, and the tug-of-war was to provide an excuse for generations of bloodshed.

Constantius' most lasting reform was to give more power to the bishops. The Church leaders got a great deal of secular authority in their regions and became an important part of the imperial political system. This modification was not always to the bishops' benefit. Constantius II was an Arian, and he made Eusebius the bishop of Constantinople. Orthodox bishops, who maintained that Christ was both fully human and fully divine, soon found they were in danger of losing their jobs through various trumped-up excuses. The Orthodox bishop of Antioch was accosted by prostitutes hired by the emperor. A number of paid witnesses gave sworn testimony that the aging bishop had bought the women's services. He was removed from office.

Religious leaders began wielding secular authority. This increase in influence was to become one of the major traits of the Middle Ages, indicating a significant break from classical culture. Traditional Romans found it unacceptable for pagan priests to have any real say over national policy, but rulers now saw that the bishops were as interested in maintaining stability and imperial authority as they were. Bishops also proved more trustworthy than generals and governors, since they would not try to set themselves up as emperor. Once Byzantium was truly established, the secular power of the clergy would begin to wane, but they would always have more influence than the pagan priests of old Rome.

Constantius II and the bishops united against the pagans. In 356, he ordered the temples closed and forbade all pagan rites. Zealous bands of Christians wrecked many shrines. It seemed the sun was setting on the old gods.

But their day had not yet ended. When Constantius II died in 361, Julian (361–63) rose to power. Julian was an emperor of a different sort. His family had been on the losing side of Constantius II's dynastic plotting. His own father was murdered by the emperor's agents. Julian was a child at the time and was spared. He spent much of his youth in exile. He was scholarly, quiet, and devoted to the classics, spending much of his time debating with pagan philosophers and reading ancient Greek books. Constantius II brought him out of exile to rule over the West when he took control from his brothers, assuming this bookish recluse would prove to be an easy pawn.

Considering Julian's isolated childhood, he showed a surprising ability for leadership. He swept through Gaul with his army, defeating the Germans and restoring order to a province that was in near anarchy. One contemporary described the state to which the region had fallen and Julian's success in restoring it: "you were going to the names of cities rather than cities, in order to create cities rather than to make use of ones that already existed."[1]

Julian had more surprises in store. While he went through the motions of being a Christian, he was secretly initiated into the sacred mysteries of Mithra. Julian believed this religion, with its combination of Greek and eastern traditions and roots in astrology and classical philosophy, could be the true unifying faith for the empire. He believed that the only way the Roman world could survive was through a reawakening of its traditional values. Christianity was an intrusion on classical culture and was responsible for the moral and spiritual decay of the people. Julian called it "a human fabrication, wrought by wickedness and devoid of any divine element."[2] Christians simply called him "Julian the Apostate."

---

1. Athanassiadi-Fowden, *Julian and Hellenism*, p. 54.
2. Ibid., pp. 165–66.

When Julian succeeded Constantius II in 361, he immediately reopened the pagan temples and restored the old sacrifices. Temples of Mithra received special favor. Christianity was too entrenched for him to ban it outright, but it lost its status as the favored religion.

Julian's religious program met with an underwhelming response. Faith in the old gods, especially among the rich and educated classes, had been eroding for two hundred years. Except for a few bastions of traditionalism such as Athens, there was no sign of the pagan Renaissance that Julian envisioned.

Julian's secular reforms were more successful. The empire suffered from tremendous debt. The ever-increasing taxes of previous years had left most individuals and many cities hopelessly in arrears. Julian forgave all outstanding debts except for those of the very wealthy, a move that endeared him to Christians and pagans alike. The cities could now spend money on defense and the rebuilding of their infrastructures. The "names of cities" became cities once again.

Then, in 363, Julian marched against the Persians. At first his campaign went well. He pushed the Sassanid armies back to the Euphrates and defeated them in front of their winter capital of Ctesiphon. At this point, Julian hesitated. Unsure if another Persian army was marching against him, he decided not to engage in a lengthy siege. He withdrew to meet up with reinforcements. The remnants of the Persian army followed him, harassing his forces all the way. In one of these skirmishes Julian was wounded by a javelin. The wound became infected, and the last pagan ruler of Rome died shortly thereafter. Some whispered that a Christian struck the blow, but the pogrom that this act could have caused never occurred. Julian's successor reversed all of his religious edicts. Christianity was once again the favored religion.

Historians dispute whether Julian would have been able to revive paganism if his rule had lasted longer. He wanted to get rid of Christianity entirely, but it is doubtful that he would have been able to do so. The cult of Mithra might have been able to replace Christianity as a state religion; it certainly did have a classical appeal. But most of the citizenry had very little classical education, or any education at all. People preferred the simple idea of a community of Christians in which one could find salvation in the afterlife for good deeds in this life over the lofty esoteric musings of the Mithraists, with their secret rites of initiation and complex astrological symbolism.

What Julian hadn't considered was the groundswell of support for Christianity in the mid- to late fourth century. As pagan temples lost their patronage and local leaders became Christians, more and more of the working people in the empire turned to the Church for leadership and inspiration. It was during this period that Christianity became the majority religion.

Christianity spread especially quickly in the empire's southern provinces: Syria, Egypt, and North Africa. Despite their regular exports of grain to Rome and Constantinople, these provinces always had been somewhat isolated intellectually. North Africa and Egypt had their own spiritual traditions; Egypt could hearken back to a glorious past of its own. But as paganism waned, Egyptians began to turn away from millennia of tradition and study the new religion. In the third century, some Egyptians formed rural communities devoted to the worship of God. Away from lingering pagan influence, they were able to devote their lives to the new faith. St. Anthony is believed to have been one of the first, establishing loosely knit communities of ascetics living in different huts or caves. Pachomius, who also operated in Egypt, founded closer organizations more like actual monasteries. The idea soon became very popular throughout Egypt. Some communities were simply religious villages, but others were restricted to men who had taken vows of chastity and poverty and lived a strict life of hard work and constant religious observance. The first Christian monasteries grew up in the land that once worshiped Isis and Osiris.

These early monks may have been inspired by stories of the great Buddhist monasteries in Asia, as well as early spiritual communities such as the Essenes, who survived in Palestine up to the second century A.D. Why Christian monasteries started in Egypt, however, remains a mystery.

The rules they set up for themselves have come down to us, carefully preserved in the libraries these communities fostered. One of the most influential was the rule of St. Benedict. The son of a Roman

Naturalistic floor mosaic from Ein Gedi, modern Israel. Nature scenes became increasingly popular as pagan themes fell out of favor.
SOURCE: Israel Ministry of Tourism.

Fourth-century Christian mosaic from Tabgha, modern Israel, showing the miracle of the loaves and fishes. Compare the quality of this fourth century mosaic, which uses large square tesserae, with the late Byzantine examples.
SOURCE: Israel Ministry of Tourism.

Another naturalistic floor mosaic from Ein Gedi, modern Israel.
SOURCE: Israel Ministry of Tourism.

nobleman, Benedict renounced his privileged life to become a hermit, later founding thirteen monasteries. Written in the early part of the sixth century, his rule is one of the earliest to survive and is still used as the basis of the Benedictine order. It was highly influential for other orders as well. Benedict went into great detail regarding how a monastic community should be run, outlining a strict but forgiving community of brothers who worked to support their own independent economy and helped each other along the spiritual path. In charge of the monks was an abbot, who was responsible for the men in his care: ·

"The abbot should always remember that he will be held accountable on Judgement Day for his teaching and the obedience of his charges. The abbot must be led to understand that any lack of good in his monks will be held as his fault. However, he will be held innocent in the Lord's judgement if he has done all within his power to overcome the corruptness and disobedience of his monks. . . . He should show them by deeds, more than by words, what is good and holy. To those who understand, he may expound verbally the Lord's directions: but to the stubborn and dull, he must exhibit the Divine commandments by his actions in his everyday life."[3]

As the monasteries attracted members and patronage, their influence increased. By the fifth century, monasticism had spread through Syria and Palestine to Anatolia. Monasteries also appeared in the West. Abbots would become powerful figures in the medieval world.

A later and stricter rule, by John of Phoberou, an influential twelfth century ascetic from western Asia Minor, warned of the temptations that could arise within the monastery itself:

"Let us instruct ourselves that whenever we meet a handsome face, whether they are our brothers or members of our

---

3. *Rule of St. Benedict*, p. 48.

Sumela Monastery, Trebizond (modern Trabzon): According to tradition this monastery was established in 386 by two holy men from Athens. Acting on a dream of the Virgin Mary telling them to found a monastery, they let a magical icon lead them to Mt. Mela near the city of Trebizond. It grew in importance throughout the Byzantine period and remained an active monastery until the early twentieth century.

SOURCE: Turkish Tourist Office.

Monastery of Mar-Saba, modern Israel. Early monasteries like this one were often built in remote locations both for defense and as a way of isolating the monks from the outside world.

SOURCE: Israel Ministry of Tourism.

own family, we do not look clearly at the handsome face, but speak looking down at the ground and in that way answer those who speak with us. For the eye of a man is like a shameless dog running in a frenzy over the faces it sees, and always the demons use this weapon against us as they also use the hand."[4]

Christianity's popularity among Egyptians was partly a result of the strong hold their pagan religion had on their consciousness. The god Osiris had gone through a process of death and resurrection not unlike the one in the story of Jesus. The goddess Isis, often shown nursing her divine infant Horus, became the model for later icons of

---

4. Jordan, "John of Phoberou," p. 69. Used by permission.

the Mother and Child. The Coptic Church, as the Egyptian church came to be called, used the *ankh*, a cross with a loop at the top instead of a bar. The ankh was an ancient religious symbol and was also the hieroglyphic word for "life." Beyond a simple word, the ankh had a spiritual resonance for the Egyptians. Their pagan religion was obsessed with the afterlife. Nearly all of its rituals were tied in some way to ensuring the worshiper a safe journey to the world beyond. This life everlasting was the promise of both the ancient ankh and the Christian cross. Early Coptic churches were decorated with ankhs. In later centuries they were replaced by crosses, but there are interesting examples of churches decorated with rows of alternating ankhs and crosses. To these early Christians, the actual shape of the cross on which Jesus was crucified was less important than the deep meaning of an ancient symbol that blended so well with the new ideology.

The Syrians developed their own brand of Christianity. While Egyptian holy men sought spiritual strength in numbers, devout Syrians wandered alone into the desert. The wastelands of Syria and Palestine had attracted spiritual seekers for millennia. Ancient accounts such as the Old Testament are full of them. They went unwashed, wearing rough clothing and with long, filthy hair. They ate whatever scraps they could beg for in the villages or the few plants they could find. They avoided human contact and were looked upon with a mixture of fear and awe by the villagers. The more traditional clergy treated them with suspicion. Benedict called them "restless, servants to the seduction of their own will and appetites."[5] John of Enchaita had a more positive view: "saints have the power of supplying what is lacking in life."[6]

One Syrian, Simeon, spent nearly forty years atop a tall pillar. The location of this strange ordeal soon became a pilgrimage center. The faithful would climb a ladder and ask him questions regarding religious matters. After his death in 459, a great church was built around the pillar, and the ruins of that church still attract pilgrims. Others followed his example, and became known as *stylites*, after the Greek word for "pillar."

---

5. *Rule of St. Benedict*, p. 47.
6. Rice, *Everyday Life in Byzantium*, p. 75.

Male head made of limestone. This Coptic work was made in Egypt in the fourth century and shows how this early Christian community was influenced by ancient Egyptian art.

Lead amulet depicting St. Simeon Stylites, twelfth century. The saint is shown emerging from the capital of a column, a halo around his head. He holds a copy of the Gospels while an angel offers him an unidentified object. Another angel holds a cross. Standing to the right and left of the column are Martha, Simeon's mother, and Conon, his disciple. The inscription reads "ulogion [blessed medallion] of St. Simeon Thaumatourgos [healer, or performer of miracles] Praise God in His saints."

SOURCE: Museum of Art and Archaeology, University of Missouri-Columbia.

Not surprisingly, these half-wild men became the subject of many miraculous tales. Simeon was renowned as a healer as well as a wise man, and many of the ascetics were credited with holy powers. The story of St. Sabas is typical.

"[St. Sabas] settled in a desert spot by the river called Gadaron, and stayed there for a short time in a cave where an enormous lion was wont to withdraw. Around midnight this lion returned and found the blessed one sleeping. Taking hold of his patchwork habit with his mouth, it began to pull at him, striving to remove him from the cave. When he got up and began the night psalmody, the lion went out and waited outside the cave; when the old man had completed the office, it came in and began to pull at him again. So, with the lion pressing him to leave the cave, the old man said to it in confidence of spirit, 'The cave is spacious enough to provide lodging for both of us, for we both have one Creator. If you want, stay here; if not, get out.' Then he adds: 'I myself was fashioned by the hand of God and privileged to receive his image.' On hearing this, the lion felt some kind of shame and withdrew."[7]

Julian's successors in the East and West were strongly pro-Christian and had little time for the musings of pagan philosophers. The temples were closed again, and the bishops were brought back into the state machinery. The western emperor Gratian (367–83) closed the temple of the Vestal Virgins in Rome, whose keeping of the Eternal Flame was once thought essential for the survival of the empire. He also removed the pagan altar from the Senate building. Paganism would linger on for many years, but it would never again have any official position. In the late fourth century, the emperors needed the Church to run much of the public infrastructure so they could concentrate on defending the frontier against a new enemy—the Huns.

---

7. *Cyril of Scythopolis, The Lives of the Monks of Palestine*, trans. R.M. Price, p. 128. Used by permission of Cistercian Publications, Inc.

The Huns terrified the Romans. While long-term contact with the Germanic tribes had made the empire gradually more tolerant of "barbarians," the Huns were a different order of barbarian altogether. Ancient writers argued over their place of origin and the reason for their sudden crossing of the frontier, but all could agree on two things—their ferocity and their smell. Ammianus Marcellinus gives a typical description.

"They wear garments of linen or of the skins of field-mice stitched together. . . . Once they have put their necks into some dingy shirt they never take it off till it rots and falls to pieces from incessant wear."[8]

Despite his disdain, Marcellinus could not help but admire the Huns' fighting skill.

"When they join battle they advance in packs, uttering their various war cries. Being lightly equipped and very sudden in their movements they can deliberately scatter and gallop about at random, inflicting tremendous slaughter; their extreme nimbleness enables them to force a rampart or pillage an enemy's camp before one catches sight of them."[9]

The Huns fell on the Goths, who were caught between the Roman Empire and the onslaught of this deadly tribe. There were two major tribes of Goths at the time, the Ostrogoths and the Visigoths. The Ostrogoths were completely conquered, while the Visigoths had no choice but to flee across the Danube River and into Roman territory.

The eastern emperor at the time, Valens (364–78), allowed the Visigoths to stay, but local Roman officials failed to provide them with the food and other aid they had been promised. Soon the Visigoths were looting the entire province in order to eat. Valens and his generals marched to stop them, spreading out in separate armies to cover

---

8. Marcellinus, *Later Roman Empire*, p. 411. Used by permission of Penguin Books, Ltd.
9. Ibid., p. 412. Used by permission of Penguin Books, Ltd.

the whole territory. For a time they were successful, or at least the generals were successful. Valens' army couldn't catch up with the Visigoths, and the victories of his subordinates began to make him look bad. Finally, at Adrianople, his scouts spotted what they said was a smaller force, camped with their families inside a circle of wagons. They were wrong. Marcellinus tells the story.

"The opposing lines came into collision like ships of war and pushed each other to and fro, heaving under the reciprocal motion like waves of the sea. Our left wing penetrated as far as the very wagons, and would have gone further if it had received any support, but it was abandoned by the rest of the cavalry, and under pressure of numbers gave way and collapsed like a broken dike. This left the infantry unprotected and so closely huddled together that a man could hardly wield his sword or draw back his arm once he had stretched it out. Dust rose in such clouds as to hide the sky, which rang with frightful shouts. In consequence it was impossible to see the enemy's missiles in flight and dodge them; all found their mark and dealt death on every side. The barbarians poured on in huge columns, trampling down horse and man and crushing our ranks as to make an orderly retreat impossible. Our men were too close-packed to have any hope of escape; so they resolved to die like heroes, faced the enemy's swords, and struck back at their assailants. On both sides helmets and breast-plates were split in pieces by blows from the battle-axe. You might see a lion-hearted savage, who had been hamstrung or had lost his right hand or been wounded in the side, grinding his clenched teeth and casting defiant glances around in the very throes of death. In this mutual slaughter so many were laid low that the field was covered with the bodies of the slain, while the groans of the dying and severely wounded filled all who heard them with abject fear."[10]

---

10. Marcellinus, *Later Roman Empire*, p. 435. Used by permission of Penguin Books, Ltd.

The Romans were surrounded and defeated. Only a third of the army escaped. Among the dead were most of the officers and Valens himself. Another province had been lost. Germanic tribes were slowly carving up the East, just as they were doing with the West.

Luckily, the next eastern emperor was Theodosius (379–95), a Spanish officer with firm Christian convictions and a great deal of military experience. When the western emperor Gratian died in 383, the region fell into disorder, with no clear leader. Theodosius favored Valentinian II among the many claimants to the title of western emperor, and dominated him until he died in 392. Then Theodosius unified the empire under his sole rule. He also waged war on the Visigoths for four years, until the war ground into a stalemate. Theodosius then offered peace, allowing the Visigoths to stay where they were, under their own kings, on the condition that they would fight alongside Roman troops if the need arose. This promise was identical to the original promise that Valens had made them.

Theodosius was a devout Christian. He presided over the second ecumenical council in 381, which established the patriarch of Constantinople as the highest Church official and tried to stamp out Arianism. Theodosius also banned pagan worship. He was one of many emperors to do so, and these repeated bans show that paganism was still alive. Theodosius wanted to get rid of the pagans once and for all. Some refused to give up their religion, and these were severely punished, some were even put to death.

He also made Orthodoxy the only recognized branch of Christianity. While this move made him many enemies among the large Arian minority, it was meant to endear him to the Orthodox hierarchy. It didn't. When the people of the Greek city of Thessaloniki murdered an unpopular army commander, Theodosius ordered the citizens massacred. The Church excommunicated him, and he was forced to publicly beg forgiveness in front of the cathedral at Milan. Humbling the emperor was a bold move on the part of the clergy, but it established the Church as having spiritual power over all Romans, no matter what their station. This led later Byzantine emperors to draw away from the pope and to put themselves at the top of the Greek Orthodox hierarchy, above even the patriarch of Constantinople.

Marble chancel screen, fifth or sixth century. In early Byzantine churches, large slabs of carved marble separated the chancel, where the altar stood, from the nave, the main body of the church where people would gather to worship. Doves and vines frame a pair of crosses in this example.

SOURCE: The Malcove Collection, University of Toronto Art Centre, Toronto, Canada.

Theodosius died in 395, leaving the empire to his two young sons, one in the East and one in the West. The split would be a permanent one. Theodosius was the last emperor to rule over an undivided Rome.

The historian Zosimus tells what happened next:

"The empire had been committed to Arcadius and Honorius, but they had authority in name only: the supreme power was held by Rufinus in the east and Stilicho in the west. . . . Wealth from all sides flowed into the households of Rufinus and Stilicho, while everywhere poverty was inflicted upon the households of those who had formerly been rich. The emperors were aware of none of these happenings, but simply signed anything Rufinus and Stilicho instructed them to sign."[11]

Rufinus and Stilicho were Germans. They had risen in the ranks of the Roman army to become powerful enough to sway the emperors themselves. That they achieved such influence was a dangerous precedent, one that would continue in the West until the very end, and which would hamper the eastern emperors for years to come.

This development might not have proven so bad if the generals had been able commanders, but they wasted much of their time vying for power and assassinating their political enemies. Stilicho, the general and real leader in the West, was successful at fighting Rome's enemies for a time, but could not stop what happened next.

In about the year 400 (the records are unclear at this point) the Visigoths, under their king Alaric, entered Italy. They brought their families along, perhaps with the intention of taking over the land as so many other tribes had done with Roman provinces. The Visigoths ravaged much of northern Italy until Stilicho met them in battle on Easter Sunday in 402. Alaric and his people were Arian Christians, and assumed that there would be no fighting that day, so they were completely surprised when Stilicho attacked. Although Stilicho was criticized for his tactic, he did manage to defeat the Visigoths. After that the campaign went badly for them, and they left Italy the next year.

The invasion did have two lasting results. The emperor Honorius moved from Milan to the well-fortified city of Ravenna. The second result was that Honorius recalled the Roman troops from the province of Britain to help protect the center of the empire. While it remained nominally a Roman province, it would soon be taken over by another group of Germans—the Anglo-Saxons.

The winter of 406 was the worst in living memory. Many froze to death and the people took it as a bad omen. It was so cold that the Rhine froze over and the Vandals, Sueves, Alans, and Burgundians

---

11. Zosimus, *Zosimus: Historia Nova*, p. 193.

crossed it and attacked Gaul. These Germanic tribes swept through the countryside for four years, eventually heading west. The provinces of Gaul and Spain began to fall under their control.

Palace intrigues led to Stilicho's assassination in 408. In the anti-German pogrom that followed, the families of the barbarian mercenaries were massacred. The soldiers flocked to Alaric, demanding vengeance. Honorius, unused to making decisions without his Germanic general, was poorly prepared to deal with the next attack.

There was little Honorius could do. His armies were not strong enough to defeat the tribes, and his provincial officials were too busy trying to defend their own territories to make any attempt to unify their forces. Alaric invaded Italy that same year, and was soon at the gates of Rome. The citizens were able to buy him off with two thousand pounds of gold, three thousand pounds of pepper (a valuable commodity at the time), and piles of silk. The next year Alaric returned, besieged the city again, and got the Senate to set up a puppet emperor. Alaric decided this arrangement wasn't so useful after all, and in 410 he returned for a third siege. This time he took the city. The emperor Honorius was safe in Ravenna, but the fall of the once-invincible capital, the symbol of the empire's glory, was a serious blow to morale. Alaric left soon after, his eyes set on conquering Africa, but he died that same year. The Visigoths settled in part of Gaul (modern France) and Spain and stayed three centuries.

The later emperors of the West struggled to control their fragmenting territory, ravaged by the Germanic migrations and perpetually split by pretenders to the throne. The situation wasn't much better in the East. The Huns raided across the Danube, getting so far that they were threatening Constantinople itself. The new eastern emperor, Theodosius II (408–50), ringed the city with massive fortifications. They saved Constantinople from the Huns, and would continue to throw off invaders for the next thousand years. The Byzantine Empire was at times the greatest power in the known world, so its wealthy capital was always a tempting prize. Constantinople would have to withstand a siege nearly every generation. The Theodosian walls would stop every foreign invader but two.

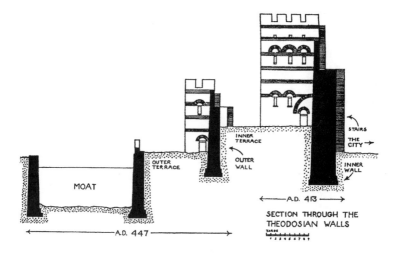

Cross section of the Theodosian land walls. Built between 412 and 447, these massive fortifications protected the capital of Byzantium for more than one thousand years.
SOURCE: *City of Constantine, 324–453,* by J.E.N. Hearsey, (John Murray Publishers, Ltd., 1963).

Theodosius II was an unlikely ruler. Quiet and scholarly, he preferred practicing calligraphy to running the affairs of state. He was dominated by his Germanic generals and his older sister Pulcheria, whom he declared empress. Byzantine tradition held that any woman could be empress. At times political necessity would call for two or more co-empresses, and there were often co-emperors as well.

Despite these problems Theodosius kept the empire safe. Unable to defeat the Huns, he bought them off. Pacifying them gave the empire the breathing space it needed to truly establish itself. Learning flourished. Theodosius II married Athenaïs Eudokia, the daughter of an Athenian professor. The emperor established a university at Constantinople, codified the laws, and encouraged talented provincials to come to the capital to learn and rise in the ranks of the court. Constantinople became the center of culture and learning that Rome once had been.

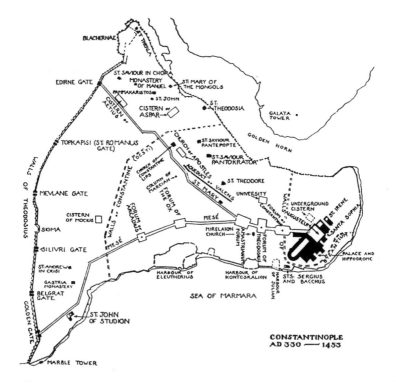

BLACHERNAE

ST SAVIOUR IN CHORA
EDIRNE GATE
MONASTERY OF MANUEL
ST MARY OF THE MONGOLS
PAMMAKARISTOS
ST JOHN
CISTERN or ASPAR
CISTERN of ASPAR→
ST THEODOSIA
GALATA TOWER
TOPKAPISI (ST ROMANUS GATE)
GOLDEN HORN
CHURCH of APOSTLES
ST SAVIOUR PANTEPOPTE
ST SAVIOUR PANTOKRATOR
CHURCH of CONSTANTINE LIPS
COLUMN of MARCIAN
ST THEODORE
AQUEDUCT of VALENS
MEVLANE GATE
ST MARY
UNIVERSITY
UNDERGROUND CISTERN
FORUM of THEODOSIUS
FORUM of THE OX
ST IRENE
SANTA SOPHIA
WALLS OF THEODOSIUS
CISTERN OF MOCIUS
MESÉ
MESÉ
SIGMA
SILIVRI GATE
MIRELAION CHURCH
ANASTRANIUM FORUM
FORUM of THEODOSIUS
FORUM of CONSTANTINE
PALACE AND HIPPODROME
ST ANDREW IN CRISI
GASTRIA MONASTERY
HARBOUR OF ELEUTHERIUS
HARBOUR OF KONTOSKALION
HARBOUR of JULIAN
STS SERGIUS AND BACCHUS
BELGRAT GATE
SEA OF MARMARA
ST JOHN OF STUDION
GOLDEN GATE

CONSTANTINOPLE
AD 330 ——— 1453

MARBLE TOWER

Map of Constantinople, showing the major monuments and landmarks.
SOURCE: *City of Constantine, 324–453,* by J.E.N. Hearsey, (John Murray Publishers, Ltd., 1963).

Theodosius II was more professor than general, but he did maintain stability. His very weakness proved an asset. The various powers behind the throne contented themselves with palace intrigues, and the emperor himself was left unmolested. There were none of the full-scale rebellions, assassination attempts, and generals marching on the capital that were so common in the West. Instead, Theodosius II died from falling off a horse.

The eastern empire had some time to recover, but many of its main problems remained unresolved. The Huns, under their famous leader Attila, were still just beyond the border, and the Germans still dominated the palace. Pulcheria selected the general Marcian (450–57) to be her husband and the new ruler. He immediately stopped paying tribute to the Huns. Everyone braced for an invasion. Amazingly, it never came. The Huns simply left, heading for easier pickings in the West. They ravaged Gaul for a time, then turned to Italy, where Attila died. His force soon disintegrated into warring factions and ceased to be a danger.

Marcian was less successful at straightening out the still-contentious issues of Christian doctrine. He tried to clarify the nature of Christ at the Council of Chalcedon in 451. At an ecumenical council in Ephesus in 431, Theodosius II had condemned the doctrine of the Nestorians, who preached that Christ was of two distinct natures— the divine and the human. This view was unpopular with those in the East, who were devoted to the Virgin Mary. If Christ were both human and divine, was Mary really the mother of God? That council had failed to end the debate, because some religious leaders were now saying that Christ had only a divine nature and was not human at all. The fourth council came to a final judgment. At Marcian's urging, the council decreed that Christ had both human and divine natures that acted together as one person. Christ was both perfectly divine and perfectly human.

The ruling pleased many Christians, but angered a large minority who thought differently. The Syrians and Egyptians, who were the main supporters of the alternative interpretations of Christ, were especially insulted. They would still be debating the nature of Christ and the status of Constantinople when they were conquered by the

Wheelcross, fifth or sixth century. The inscriptions read, "for the sake of salvation and succour . . . life . . . light."
SOURCE: Museum of Art and Archaeology, University of Missouri-Columbia.

Muslims two centuries later. The Nestorians didn't accept the judgment either. Although their influence in Byzantium was at an end, they set off to proselytize far to the east, making it all the way to China and Mongolia.

Solving the German problem fell to the next eastern emperor, Leo (457–74). He owed his position to influential Germans at court, but he immediately started plotting their downfall. First he sent for some soldiers from Isauria, a region in Asia Minor that was famed for its fighting men. He married his daughter off to their chieftain Zeno and made the troops his personal bodyguard. The Isaurians then proceeded to massacre all the powerful Germans in the palace. The message was clear—provincials could be the power behind the throne, but Germans could not.

The Isaurians would become more than that. When Leo died in 474, Zeno became emperor. From then on, Isaurians would be some of the empire's greatest generals and rulers. Foreigners would not hold sway over Byzantine emperors for many years.

In the West, the emperors now exercised little power outside of Italy. Germanic tribes had all but taken over Gaul and Spain. German generals decided who would succeed to the throne. North Africa, once the breadbasket of Rome, was now a Vandal kingdom, and Britain had been abandoned for two generations.

Then, in 476, the inevitable happened. The western emperor Romulus Augustulus was deposed by Odoacer, the leader of his German troops. The emperor was only sixteen. He had never really ruled and was not enough of a threat for Odoacer to bother killing him. Instead, Odoacer gave the boy a pension and allowed him to retire to the countryside, where he spent the rest of his days founding churches and supporting monasteries. Odoacer proclaimed himself king and asked the eastern emperor Zeno (474–91) to recognize him as the new emperor of the West. Zeno refused, but was too busy securing his own borders to retake Italy. To save face, Zeno granted him the title of patrician. The Roman administration of Italy continued to function under Odoacer, who retained the chief officers of state, but the year 476 is generally considered the end of the Roman Empire of the West.

The importance of the "fall" of the Roman Empire is easily exaggerated. The historian Averil Cameron called it "one of the most famous non-events in history." [12] The deposing of Augustulus made official what everyone already knew. The last emperors of the West, and there were many, five in the ten years leading up to 476, were nothing but puppets. Italy was already a Germanic kingdom. The western provinces were breaking up into separate states. The Franks would go on to found the Merovingian dynasty, the first rulers of what would become France. The Visigoths would create a new nation in Spain. The Angles, Saxons, and Jutes would found the kingdoms of Anglo-Saxon England. If the date 476 has any importance, it is only as a milestone on the road to medieval and modern Europe.

---

12. Cameron, *Mediterranean World in Late Antiquity*, p. 33.

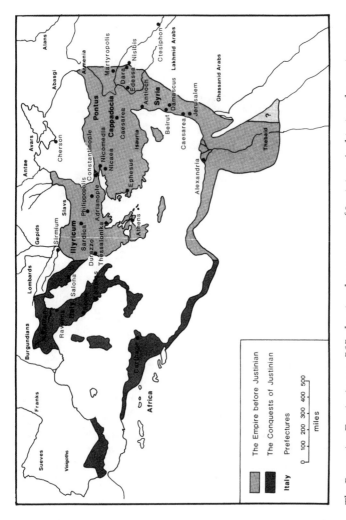

The Byzantine Empire in A.D. *565, showing the conquests of Justinian. At this time the empire was at its greatest geographical extent.*

SOURCE: *Byzantium: An Introduction to East Roman Civilization,* N. Baynes and H. Moss, eds. (Clarendon Press, an imprint of Oxford University Press, 1961). Used by permission of Oxford University Press.

III.

AN EMPIRE WON AND LOST

(476–695)

=⇒◆⇐=

The Roman Empire had lost half its inheritance. A solution was needed, or the East would go the way of the West. The resourceful emperor Zeno hit upon an idea that would solve both the problems of the Ostrogoths in Thrace, who had broken away from the Huns and were now harassing his frontier, and Odoacer in Italy. He made a truce with Theodoric, king of the Ostrogoths. In return for peace, Zeno would support them as they migrated to Italy. There they would defeat Odoacer and rule the peninsula as a vassal state. Soon the Germans in Italy had to fight an immigration problem of their own. Odoacer's armies proved no match for the influx of the Ostrogoths, and soon he was suing for peace.

Odoacer offered what he thought was a good deal—he and Theodoric would share power and rule together from the palace at Ravenna, northern Italy. The Ostrogothic king agreed, but at a feast shortly thereafter, he leapt out of his seat, drew his sword, and cut Odoacer nearly in half. When he saw how completely he had dispatched his rival, the Goth is said to have exclaimed "The wretch cannot have had a bone in his body!"[1]

Theodoric kept his promise to Zeno and ruled Italy in the emperor's name. It proved both profitable and easy. The Roman population was still a strong force there, and they were happy to be part

---

1. Norwich, *Short History of Byzantium*, p. 56.

of the empire again and to have their property and families secure. Theodoric had spent much of his early life in Constantinople as a guest of the imperial court, and so was familiar with Roman laws and customs. He allowed the Romans in his territory to live under Roman law, while his Ostrogoths lived under Gothic law.

Throughout his reign, Zeno had problems with the Church. The Council of Chalcedon did little to solve the debate over Christ's nature. Monophytism, the idea that Christ had only one inseparable divine nature, was becoming popular among common people and even the pope himself. The doctrine gained the most support in Syria, Egypt, and Armenia, the areas where Greek influence was at its weakest. The Orthodox faction, supported by the Greeks and upper classes, especially in the capital, proclaimed that Christ was both God and man.

These seem like fine distinctions, but to the Byzantines they were of the utmost importance. Only through a belief that was pure and completely correct could there be any hope of salvation. Any deviation from the Truth meant eternal damnation. The problem was, the Truth was bound up in the complex language of the Bible. Monophytism would not be the last controversy in the Church.

Zeno and Acacius, the patriarch of Constantinople, reiterated the declaration of the council. When the pope heard this he was infuriated—he, not the patriarch, should have the final say on Church matters. He excommunicated Acacius. The person who was supposed to give a copy of the pope's decree to the strong-willed patriarch was so afraid of being the bearer of bad news that he crept up behind Acacius in the middle of a service and pinned it to the back of his cloak. When Acacius finally discovered this ecclesiastical "kick me" sign, he immediately excommunicated the pope. These excommunications signaled the first formal rift between the eastern and western Churches. The two groups of Christians were beginning to head down different paths, ones that would lead to the modern Catholic and Greek Orthodox Churches.

When Zeno died in 491, he was succeeded by the conservative and thrifty Anastasius (491–518). Before Anastasius became emperor he had been an outspoken monophysite, but he signed a pledge of

The church of St. Ripsime in Armenia. Completed in 618, it is dedicated to a fourth-century female saint who was martyred for preaching Christianity. The building, like Armenian architecture in general, shows Byzantine influence.

SOURCE: School of Architecture, College of Architecture, Planning, and Landscape Architecture, University of Arizona.

Orthodoxy in order to expedite his path to the throne. He couldn't hide his true feelings, however, and soon was favoring the monophysites and banishing Orthodox leaders. There were riots in the streets, and it looked for a while as if the emperor would lose his throne, but he gave a rallying speech in the Hippodrome in which he offered to relinquish his title. The gamble worked. The populace realized that they needed a stable government. Anastasius kept his position.

The people made the right choice. Anastasius managed the economy so well that by the end of his reign the imperial treasury was filled with 23 million gold coins, three times the empire's annual budget. He did this by firing many well-paid but essentially useless courtiers. The Isaurians went too. They had served their purpose. He cut back on other expenses as well, and even auctioned off Zeno's clothes.

During this time a new power arose in the capital. After Constantine banned gladiator fights, the people had turned to chariot races for entertainment. These were only slightly less bloody. Charioteers would often whip their opponents as much as their horses and would try every trick they could get away with to make the other teams crash. Deaths were commonplace, but the people loved the excitement of the races and the spectacle of the Hippodrome decorated with colorful banners and streamers. Charioteers became stars. The Hippodrome became the center of entertainment and a popular meeting place. Large fan clubs rallied behind the best teams. The four principal ones were the Blues, the Greens, the Whites, and the Reds, named after the colors the charioteers and fans wore. The fans worked themselves into such a furor during the games that they often ended up rioting. Fights in the Hippodrome were frequent. Some devoted fans even turned to black magic. Archaeologists have discovered lead tablets inscribed with curses against rival teams.

Sometime in the late fifth or early sixth century the two most important factions, the Blues and the Greens, were granted political powers. Their near-monopoly of the games brought them both prestige and a great amount of money, but now they were given the responsibility of defending and maintaining the city walls. With real power added to their wealth, they soon became important political parties.

Anastasius died in 518 without naming an heir. Soon all of Constantinople was plotting to get their own candidates on the throne. A noblewoman handed Justin, a commander of the palace guard, a huge sum of money to give to his troops so they would hail her candidate as the new emperor. Justin doled out the money, but didn't pass on her message. The soldiers assumed the money was from him and declared him their ruler.

Justin (518–27) was born a peasant, herded pigs in his youth, and joined the army to better himself. While a soldier he met an attractive slave named Lupicina. Lupicina's master enjoyed her company, but nevertheless sold her to Justin, who promptly freed and married her. Anastasius recognized and rewarded talent, and Justin was able to rise up the ranks until he reached a position of influence. While opportunities changed depending on who was on the throne, there was always a fair amount of upward mobility in Byzantine society. Those who were capable, useful, and ruthless could go from very humble beginnings to the highest positions.

Justin and Lupicina were avowed supporters of Orthodoxy, but they managed to smooth over relations with Rome enough to bring about a reconciliation, ending thirty-five years of schism. While the imperial couple ruled well, the real power behind the throne was Justin's nephew Justinian, a brilliant and ambitious soldier who rose in the ranks with his uncle.

If Justin's choice of a wife was questionable, Justinian's was scandalous. He fell in love with a young actress of the Blues faction named Theodora. Actresses in Roman times were not considered respectable citizens. They would perform any sort of play, from ancient Greek tragedies to productions of a more earthy variety. If modern starlets acted in similar fashion, they would perform both in Hollywood blockbusters and cheap pornography. Theodora's exploits on the stage were legendary and were meticulously recorded by Procopius, the court historian, in his *Secret History*. As the name suggests, this book was never published in Justinian's and Theodora's lifetime, and reads like the angry diatribe of an alienated employee:

> "She was the kind of comedienne who delights the audience
> by letting herself be cuffed and slapped on the cheeks, and

makes them guffaw by raising her skirts to reveal to the spec-
tators those feminine secrets here and there which custom
veils from the eyes of the opposite sex. . . . On the field of
pleasure she was never defeated. Often she would go pic-
nicking with ten young men or more, in the flower of their
strength and virility, and dallied with them all, the whole
night through. When they wearied of the sport, she would
approach their servants, perhaps thirty in number, and fight
a duel with each of these; and even thus found no allayment
of her craving."[2]

When Justin died Justinian (527–65) took over. He and
Theodora ruled in style, hosting magnificent public games and
launching a lavish building program. The treasury that Anastasius
had so prudently filled was soon empty. Justinian's tax collectors
scoured the empire for funds. While the poor could content themselves knowing that the rich were being squeezed as much as
everyone else, that knowledge didn't keep them from being jailed and
tortured if the collectors thought they were holding out. In his never-
ending quest for money and power, Justinian made several reforms
that would have lasting significance. First, he codified all the old
Roman laws, which made the government run far more efficiently. He
also took power away from provincial officials and put it into the
hands of the central government.

The vacuum of power in the provinces was quickly filled by local
Church leaders who consolidated their hold on the daily lives of citizens. The bishops had already gained a great deal of secular power
under Constantius II, and now their main rivals for local power were
gone. But unlike in the west, they did not have a pope as their ulti-
mate authority. Instead, they had the patriarch of Constantinople
and, above him, the emperor. At this time the pope still had some
sway, but the emperor was the real head of the Church in the East.
This was one of the unique aspects of the Byzantine system of government. Generally, the emperor did not interfere in religious affairs,

---

2. Procopius, *Secret History,* pp. 46–47. Used by permission of the University of
Michigan Press.

Retinue of Empress Theodora, 547 A.D.   Emperor Justinian (482–565)   Empress Theodora (d. 548)

Nineteenth-century rendering of Justinian and Theodora and their retinues.
SOURCE: *Historic Costume in Pictures*, by Braun & Schneider (Dover Publications, Inc., 1975).

leaving most decisions to the patriarch, and the religious hierarchy did not interfere in politics. There are numerous instances in Byzantine history where this system did not work, but it was the ideal to which most rulers aspired.

The Church was becoming increasingly wealthy in the fifth and sixth centuries, and there was a gradual rift appearing between the common people and their religion. While the fifth century had been a time of religious eclecticism, the sixth was a time of entrenchment into well-established sects. Gone were the days when hermits and ascetics could attract pilgrims from across the empire. In the fifth century, pilgrims could go and see Saint Simeon atop his column, dispensing wisdom and arousing faith through his self-sacrifice. A century later, they had to satisfy themselves by going to the great church that had been built around his pillar. They could pray for miracles at the dead saint's bones, but Simeon had left few heirs to continue his message.

East end of the Basilica of Bishop Euphrasius, Poreč, Croatia, c. 550. A basilica is a simple rectangular structure with rows of windows high on the walls to admit light. Columns run the length of the building to support the roof and divide the structure into several aisles. The basilica was a late Roman form used for commercial and legal buildings and was adopted as a style for early churches. The conch, the half-dome at the end of the basilica, stood above the altar. The mosaics here show several popular motifs, such as the enthroned Christ flanked by apostles, and the Virgin and child with angels, a local martyr, and a patron offering a model of the church.

SOURCE: Robert Ousterhout.

Theodora initiated some reforms of her own. Becoming an empress seems to have truly changed her. She broke away from her past and became a capable ruler in her own right. She established a shelter for reformed prostitutes and caused a law to be passed to guarantee a woman's right to her dowry. In the Hippodrome, the Blues and Greens struggled for dominance. Procopius wrote that the fighting now spilled out into the streets:

"Almost all of them carried steel openly . . . by day they concealed their two-edged daggers along the thigh of their cloaks. Collecting in gangs as soon as dusk fell, they robbed their betters in the open Forum and in the narrow alleys, snatching from passersby their mantles, belts, gold brooches, and whatever they had in their hands."

"Now at first they killed only their opponents. But as matters progressed, they also murdered men who had done nothing against them. And there were many who bribed them with money, pointing out personal enemies, whom the Blues straightway dispatched, declaring these victims were Greens, when as a matter of fact they were utter strangers."[3]

Justinian's reign saw the rise of the emperor as a supreme autocrat. The central government had more power than ever before, as the people of Constantinople would learn to their regret.

In 532, the people had finally had enough of Justinian's heavy-handedness. The previous year several members of the Blues and Greens had been arrested for murder and sentenced to hang. Their sentences had been commuted, but that wasn't enough for the two factions; they wanted the prisoners freed. During a chariot race in the Hippodrome, the Blues and the Greens chanted *"Nika! Nika!"* ("Victory! Victory!"). Soon the cheer changed from encouragement of their teams into a call for Justinian to pardon the prisoners, then it quickly changed to a call for overthrowing of the government. Both factions

---

3. Procopius, *Secret History,* p. 36. Used by permission of the University of Michigan Press.

had a new definition of victory—the overthrow of Justinian. The fans poured out of the Hippodrome and ransacked the homes of Justinian's supporters. For five days mobs ruled the streets, attacking officials, opening the jails, and burning down public buildings. In this they were influenced by members of the Senate, who disapproved of Justinian's high taxes and his lessening of the nobility's power. The mob grabbed Hypatius, a nephew of the old emperor Anastasius, and put him on Justinian's seat at the Hippodrome.

Justinian hid in his palace, unsure what to do. Theodora mocked him, saying, ". . . how could an emperor ever allow himself to be a fugitive? May I myself never willingly shed my imperial robes, nor see the day when I am no longer addressed by my title. If you, my lord, wish to save your skin, you will have no difficulty in doing so. As for me, I stand by the ancient saying: 'the purple is the noblest winding sheet.'"[4]

That was too much for Justinian to bear. He sent in the army. The soldiers corralled the rioters into the Hippodrome and massacred them. When it was all over, thirty thousand people lay dead and Hypatius was trembling at Justinian's feet. The emperor had him executed and his body thrown into the sea, and then banished the senators who had encouraged the riot. The revolt made Justinian scale back on some of his policies, lowering taxes and curbing the greatest excesses of his collectors, but he left no one in doubt of who was in control.

Among the many buildings destroyed in the riots was the church of St. Sophia. Recognizing that it was the most popular church in the city, Justinian rebuilt it in style, completing it in 537. The new edifice was much larger than the old and featured an immense golden dome surrounded at its base by windows. When the sun shone through, the glare made the thin pillars between the windows disappear, so that the dome seemed to hover in the air. The interior was richly furnished with gold, porphyry, and gemstones. Many priceless relics were on display: the True Cross, the table from the Last Supper, even Christ's baby clothes. Later rulers added intricate mosaics showing

---

4. Norwich, *Short History of Byzantium*, p. 64.

Hagia Sophia, Constantinople: View from the second-story balcony. The roundels with Arabic writing were added by the Ottoman Turks when they converted the church into a mosque.

Hagia Sophia, Constantinople: View from the ground floor.
SOURCE: School of Architecture, College of Architecture, Planning, and Landscape Architecture, University of Arizona.

Hagia Sophia, Constantinople: Aerial view. The Bosphorus is in the background. The minarets were added in the Ottoman period when the church was converted into a mosque.

SOURCE: Turkish Tourist Office.

emperors, Jesus, and the Virgin Mary against a heavenly background of pure gold. Named Hagia Sophia, "the Church of Holy Wisdom," it became the artistic and social centerpiece of the capital. The bloodiest riot in the history of Constantinople led to the creation of its greatest landmark.

Justinian now set his sights on the west. He dreamed of making all the Mediterranean, from the Bosphorus to the Straits of Gibraltar, Roman again. His first target was North Africa, a province rich in grain. It was now ruled by the Vandals, a Germanic tribe that had marched all the way from the Rhine across Europe, then south into Africa. This farthest extent of the Germanic migration was not to last. Justinian sent his loyal general Belisarius (who was also married to an "actress") with a large fleet manned by experienced troops and Hun mercenaries. The Vandals had never experienced a Hunnic cavalry charge and were routed in two decisive engagements.

Belisarius wisely kept his Huns in check. He treated the North Africans as what they had always considered themselves to be— Roman citizens. This benediction didn't stop Belisarius from hauling back the Vandals' royal treasury, including the menorah and other furnishings that had been taken from the Hebrew Temple in Jerusalem by the emperor Titus after its destruction in A.D. 70. An earlier Vandal king had stolen them from Rome and brought them to North Africa. The Jewish community in Jerusalem begged to have them returned, and Justinian complied.

Belisarius then sailed to Italy. Justinian didn't want to share power with the Ostrogoths. He planned to have the peninsula reinstated as a full province. Taking advantage of a bloody fight for succession to the Gothic throne, Belisarius was able to take Sicily, cross to the mainland, and start fighting his way north. This time Belisarius didn't restrain himself and looted the towns and villages along the way. The Ostrogoths fled before him and he marched into Rome unopposed.

Then the Ostrogoths counterattacked and Belisarius was trapped inside the city walls. A grueling siege ensued during which the Roman army and the much-reduced population starved inside, while the Ostrogoths died of disease outside. Belisarius' men nearly perished from hunger before another Byzantine force saved them. The two armies then launched a long and hard-fought campaign that eventually won them all of Italy. But victory came at a price. The countryside was ravaged, Rome was nearly depopulated, and Milan was nothing more than a smoking ruin. Justinian ruled over Italy, but not an Italy anyone from the old days of the empire would have recognized.

Just as the day was won in the western regions, disaster struck at home. In 540, the Persian king Chosroes I invaded Asia Minor and plundered Antioch, the second largest city in the empire. He sold the city back for five thousand pounds of gold.

Chosroes was an absolute ruler. The Persian, or Sassanid, empire was tightly controlled and highly organized. His philosophy of government was simple: "The monarchy depends on the army, the army on money; money comes from the land-tax; the land-tax comes from agriculture. Agriculture depends on justice, justice on the integrity of officials, and integrity and reliability on the ever-watchfulness of the King."[5]

The Persian empire had a highly centralized system of government, with far more control over its subjects than the old Roman Empire. Every house and patch of land was accounted for. The Byzantines admired the efficiency of the Sassanid state and imitated it. Byzantium became increasingly centralized, until the government controlled virtually every aspect of life. Many industries became state monopolies. Accurate censuses were taken to ensure efficient taxation. Even charity was systematized. While Byzantium owed its spirit to classical Greece and Rome, it owed a great deal of its system of government to the Persians.

Shortly after Byzantium's humiliating defeat at the hands of the Sassanid Persians, the bubonic plague swept across the eastern Mediterranean. Epidemics had always been a problem, especially in the crowded and dirty cities, but the Romans had never seen bubonic plague before. This latest outbreak would last for decades, and by the time it passed nearly a third of the entire population was dead.

Justinian himself contracted the disease and was bedridden for the better part of a year. Theodora ruled in his place, but there was nothing she could do to stop the deadly epidemic. The barbarian peoples, who lived in less populated conditions than the city-dwellers of Byzantium and Persia, were less affected by the disease. Once again barbarians harassed the borders. Persia, also weakened by the plague, was nonetheless able to gather enough troops to eject the Byzantines from Armenia. The country would change hands several more times, but its loss was always a blow to prestige. Despite this, Justinian was more concerned with consolidating his hold on the west. These areas were traditionally Roman and to regain them would make him very popular.

Belisarius was sent back to Italy. The entire province was in revolt. The Romans were tiring of Justinian's heavy taxes and handed many of the cities back to the Ostrogoths. Rome held out, but was

5. Brown, Peter, *The World of Late Antiquity*, p. 166. Used by kind permission of Thames & Hudson, Ltd. © 1987.

under siege. Belisarius tried to save it and failed. The Ostrogoths took it and looted what few valuables were left in the once-great city. In 549, Belisarius returned to Constantinople, leaving Italy divided between Byzantines and Ostrogoths.

During this time Italy was becoming less and less important, in part due to the increasing devastation of the countryside. It was no longer the rich province it had once been. Even the luster of Rome itself was tarnished. Since 410 it had been taken and sacked numerous times. Many of its great buildings were abandoned. The palaces of the senators had become dwelling places for squatters and refugees. The universities were closed. The Forum was little more than a country marketplace choked with weeds. Rome was no longer the center of the world, merely a sad reminder of an age that was no more. Now Constantinople was the Immortal City.

But still Justinian did not give up. In 552, a Byzantine army would again sail to Italy, this time under the command of a eunuch named Narses. The Ostrogoths had set themselves up in Rome, and by many accounts were running the city and countryside better than Justinian ever had. Narses eventually won the campaign and the Ostrogoths were permanently expelled from Italy.

Justinian regained the west, but at a price. Italy was in ruins and the treasury was empty. His building campaign stopped and the army began to shrink. The empire was there, but the money required to run it was not.

When Justinian died in 565, he was succeeded by his nephew Justin II (565–78). The new emperor promised to curb the over-spending that had so weakened the economy. His first act was to stop paying the ruinous tribute his uncle used to buy peace with the empire's enemies. However, the money saved wasn't enough to buy a decent army. When the Avars, a well-organized Turkic people, invaded the province of Dalmatia, modern Albania and Yugoslavia, the army was not able to defeat them. Justin was forced to restore the tribute at a higher rate.

There was also a long and tiring war with Persia. The fight was over border territories and also to help the Armenians. The Armenians had rebelled when the Persians tried to set up a Zoroastrian fire temple near the church of their patriarch. Justin II wanted to help his fellow Christians, but the war went badly. The Persians raided deep into Byzantine-controlled Syria and eventually forced the emperor to pay an annual tribute in exchange for peace.

In the west, a small Germanic tribe called the Lombards migrated into north and central Italy from 568–72. They meshed with the local population and stole, bought, or married into vast estates, setting themselves up as a rural aristocracy. While they eventually became Christians and learned to speak Latin, they had no interest in being ruled by the emperor in Constantinople. They remained fiercely independent until conquered by Charlemagne two hundred years later. The region of Lombardy was one of their strongholds and still preserves their name.

Pair of Germanic fibulae dating from around 550 to 600. These clasps were used to hold cloaks and other clothing and were a typical ornament of the German tribes. These examples are made of gilded bronze.

SOURCE: Museum of Art and Archaeology, University of Missouri-Columbia.

The strain of these repeated setbacks left Justin II a mental wreck. The windows of the palace were fitted with bars to keep him from leaping to his death. His courtiers wheeled him along the halls in a cart while musicians played soothing music. His successor Tiberius Constantine (578–82) was not much better. His spending program rivaled Justinian's in wastefulness. He gave away more than seven thousand pounds of gold as gifts and lowered taxes for everyone by 25 percent. He died after only four years on the throne, perhaps by poisoning, and his able general Maurice took power.

Maurice (582–602) was the leader Byzantium desperately needed. His stable reign lasted twenty years, during which he did a great deal to strengthen the empire's position. He was able to help a usurper onto the Persian throne in exchange for the return of Armenia and Mesopotamia. But his tight-fisted economic policies brought him trouble. Where Tiberius Constantine had been generous to a fault, Maurice was obsessively cheap. He made the army camp out during the winter to spare him the cost of paying for them to return home, and he curtailed much of the public charity. He was deposed in favor of one of the worst leaders in Byzantium's eleven-hundred-year history—Phokas.

Phokas (602–10) is a perfect example of why power should never be put in the hands of a single person. A heavy drinker, he left only two legacies to his reign—one meaningless and the other cruel. The first was his habit of wearing a beard. Romans were traditionally clean-shaven. Only "barbarians" had facial hair. But as Byzantium drifted further away from its Roman roots, fashions started to change. After Phokas, most emperors sported beards, some reaching down to their waist.

Perhaps the Byzantines should have kept their razors, for the other legacy of Phokas truly was barbaric. The emperor instituted torture as a regular means of justice. Phokas was an enthusiastic supporter of torture and seemed to enjoy it as a bizarre fetish. In front of his eager eyes, people accused of crimes would be flogged, or have their ears and noses hacked off. Others were flayed alive. The emperor delighted in inventing new horrors to mete out on his prisoners, the more cruel and unusual the better. After Phokas, the

Byzantine system of justice became a nightmare of mutilations and executions.

While Phokas was amusing himself at the expense of his citizens, the frontiers were collapsing. The Avars joined with the Slavs and overran the Balkans. They reached the gates of Constantinople, but the walls stopped them. The Slavs settled in the region south of the Danube and never left. They eventually assimilated into the empire, but they have kept their identity to this day. The Turks, who had never before been considered a threat, suddenly invaded Crimea. The Persians ravaged Asia Minor and camped within sight of the capital.

At this point the governor of Carthage, a man named Herakleios, sailed to Constantinople and declared himself emperor. Herakleios had lost a battle and felt that a coup attempt would be safer than reporting his failure to his demented ruler. No one lifted a finger to save Phokas. The tyrant was dragged in front of Herakleios, who cursed him for bringing so much suffering to the empire. Phokas took the abuse calmly, then asked him if he was sure he could do any better. His head was lopped off and his body was burned in front of a cheering crowd.

Phokas' question took some time to answer. Herakleios (610–41) was an able ruler, but he took on a serious situation. In the early years of his reign, the Persians took all the land between Antioch and Egypt. The capture of Egypt was a heavy blow, since it was an important source of grain. Jerusalem was an even worse loss. The True Cross had been moved there from Constantinople some time before, and now it was carried off by the pagan Sassanids.

Herakleios focused all his energies on defeating Byzantium's greatest enemy. He made peace with the Avars and confiscated money from corrupt officials to finance the upcoming war. The people rallied to his cause. The Church melted down gold chalices and plates to buy weapons and provisions.

His greatest innovation was the *theme* system. Since the army was short of men, he attracted recruits by offering land on the frontier. In exchange for this land the men were required to fight. Since they now had a personal stake in the region, they generally fought better than the standing army. It is unclear if Herakleios formulated the system completely or if he came up with the original idea and it developed slowly over time, but once it was established it worked efficiently and was used for centuries. In later years, Slavs were offered the deal as well. This system helped pacify them and bring them into Byzantine society.

In 622, he marched east. What followed was the greatest series of victories since the days of Belisarius. Herakleios was a charismatic and brilliant leader. Fortunately for the Byzantines, the Persian leader, Chosroes II, was the exact opposite. Chosroes' mind was slowly breaking, and he gave strange and occasionally incomprehensible commands to his generals. Trying to win the war, his officers generally ignored him, but that was a dangerous move. When one of his generals died shortly after a defeat, the mad king had his body packed in salt and shipped to the palace at Ctesiphon. There he watched as the corpse was tortured and hacked to bits as a punishment for its incompetence in life.

Despite this lack of leadership, the Persians fought hard. One army was able to slip around the advancing Byzantines and besiege Constantinople. The Slavs joined them, hoping the vast Sassanid army could succeed where they had failed. The city's populace, as they would do so many times in Byzantine history, pushed back wave after wave of attackers. The patriarch rallied them by marching along the ramparts with an icon of the Virgin. Then the Byzantine navy surprised the invader's fleet. Neither the Persians nor the Slavs were used to fighting on the sea, while the Greeks had been doing so since the days of Homer. Soon the Bosphorus was filled with wrecked ships and floating bodies.

At about this time, both the Persian and the Byzantine rulers received letters from an obscure religious leader named Muhammad. He was the founder of a new faith called Islam in the backwater land of Arabia, a place so barren that in all the wars fought between Byzantium and Persia, neither side had ever bothered invading it. The letters invited them to convert to his religion. There is no record that either leader took the time to send a reply.

Meanwhile Herakleios was marching on the Persian palace at Ctesiphon. A Persian army rode out to meet him. In the ensuing melee, which lasted eleven hours, the Persian general challenged the Byzantine emperor to single combat. Although he was already bleeding from several wounds, Herakleios rode through the struggling soldiers and sliced off the general's head with a single cut of his sword.

The battle turned into a slaughter. Herakleios burned the palace to the ground. Chosroes II fled but was captured and tortured to death by his own son. The Persians then sued for peace. The holy relics and all of Byzantium's lost territories were returned. The Persians would be a serious threat to the Byzantine Empire no more.

Herakleios marched in triumph into Constantinople, the True Cross held aloft before him as his subjects fell to their knees and thanked God for their victory. The Cross was set in front of the altar at the Hagia Sophia and the entire populace celebrated.

Peace was not to last. In 633 the Arabs burst out of the desert, inflamed with an unstoppable zeal for their new religion of Islam. Their prophet Muhammad had died the year before. Now they were ruled by his "caliph," or representative. They descended on Syria and took the province in a series of whirlwind attacks.

Syria was an easy target. Although recently taken back from Persia, Byzantine's hold on the region was weak. Furthermore, the Semitic peoples there felt some sympathy for the Arabs. The strict monotheism of Islam, which rejected the concept of the Trinity, was more in accord with their monophysite beliefs than the Orthodoxy of Constantinople. The Arabs also offered tolerance and an end to the constant religious wrangling that had typified so much of the politics under Byzantine rule. Jews and Christians were allowed to worship in any way they saw fit, as long as they paid a special tax for the privilege.

The Arabs took Palestine as easily as they took Syria. Jerusalem held out for a time, but with no relieving army in sight, it reluctantly surrendered in 640. The Arab general Omar rode into the city dressed all in white, as if he was on pilgrimage. His first stop was the site of the ancient Temple Mount. There the Prophet Muhammad was said to have risen from the altar of Abraham up into Heaven to see the pleasures of the afterlife. Omar built a small mosque there, which was eventually replaced by the Mosque of Omar, the golden-domed edifice that is still the centerpiece of Jerusalem's skyline.

Herakleios had defeated Byzantium's most powerful enemy, only to have his gains lost to an almost unknown people. He died in 641, a broken man. His successors fared little better. The Arabs soon took Egypt and much of North Africa. Again, there were few Byzantine forces in the region, the large armies all being massed on the Persian or Balkan borders. Local garrisons fought for a time, but they had little chance against the Arabs, who by all accounts fought with ferocity and a contempt for life, even their own. Alexandria, the most Greek of all the cities in Africa, was the last to fall. A Byzantine fleet retook it for a time, but accomplished nothing besides teaching the Arabs the value of owning a navy. The shipyards of Alexandria and Syria began building Islam's first fleet. The ships were built and manned by local crews, the Arabs having no experience with such things, and soon the Arabs were defeating the Byzantines on sea as well as land.

While Emperor Constans II (641–68) tried to stem the tide, the debate over Christ's nature was reaching such proportions that another schism seemed inevitable. The pope said that belief in the dual nature of Christ was heresy and must be abolished, and the emperor insisted that the whole thing be forgotten for the sake of unity. Constans II did the only thing he could do: he had the pope thrown in prison and put a more pliable pontiff on the throne of St. Peter.

The Arabs took Egypt in 642, and Byzantium lost one of its richest provinces forever. The Arabs then turned on Mesopotamia, which was divided up between Byzantium and Persia. Despite being a war zone for the better part of a century, there were very few troops there. The Byzantine forces had been recently withdrawn to deal with the Slavic threat, and the Persian forces were scattered and all but leaderless. The defeat that Herakleios had inflicted on the Persians revealed just how weak and tyrannical their rulers were. The capital had little authority now, and many parts of the Persian empire were basically autonomous regions. The Arabs rode into this power vacuum and soon were masters of the region.

Once again, the people seemed not to mind. The Arabs, although they were conquerors, at least brought stability. The Jews and Christians were allowed to keep their faith in exchange for the special tax. The cities, too, had to pay tribute, but the Arab empire had very little infrastructure to support. The money they took, while a fortune in the eyes of desert nomads, was a pittance compared to the burdensome taxes imposed by the unwieldy state apparatus of Byzantium or Persia.

Persia was gone in a few years. While the Sassanid army put up a brave resistance, province after province fell into the hands of the Muslims. The Persian king was never able to rally his forces, and the rapidity of the Arab advance is testament to just how exhausted the Persian economy was after so many years of war with Byzantium.

In 674, the Arabs attacked Constantinople. They brought a large fleet of ships burdened with giant catapults that the Arabs hoped would batter down the walls. The Arabs had yet to suffer a serious defeat, and it looked like the city might finally fall. But the defenders had a secret weapon. When the Arabian fleet sailed close to the walls to use their catapults, great gouts of flame emerged from strange devices positioned on the ramparts. The fire spread over the decks and rigging, setting everything alight. The crews desperately tried to extinguish it, but water did nothing but spread the flames. Soon the surface of the sea itself was on fire. The Arabs retreated in panic. They had received their first experience with Greek fire, a mysterious substance that has baffled modern scholars. It seems to have been some sort of petroleum gel that was squirted out of a set of bellows, basically an early form of napalm.

Although this primitive flamethrower terrified the Arabs, they were not about to give up. They besieged the city for five years but were unable to breach the walls. By the time they left, their army had been decimated and their once-proud fleet was all but gone. The Arab advance finally stopped. If it had not been for the thick walls of Theodosius and the deadly weapon of some forgotten inventor, the Arab invasion might have swept through all of Europe, radically changing world history.

71

A nineteenth-century reconstruction of the Theodosian Walls of Constantinople.
SOURCE: School of Architecture, College of Architecture, Planning, and Landscape Architecture, University of Arizona.

Constantinople could not rest, however. A new enemy, the Bulgars, appeared north of the Danube. They were a mixed race of Turkic and Hunnic stock. They were pagans, with a society made up of clans ruled over by a single khan and his aristocracy. These pastoral nomads slowly melded with the Slavs, who greatly outnumbered them, but managed to keep much of their culture intact. Like the Goths and Huns before them, they were soon crossing the Danube into imperial territory. The Byzantines, worn out from defeating first the Persians and then the Arabs, simply bought them off. Dishonor was cheaper than war. The Bulgars set up an independent state on Byzantine soil in 681. Byzantium recognized this state, but the empire would never cede its claim to the land. This conflict would be a cause of many future wars.

Now that there was a semblance of stability, the argument over the nature of Christ was finally resolved. In 681, an ecumenical council determined that God had "two natural wills and two natural energies, without division, alteration, separation, or confusion."[6] Anyone who disagreed was excommunicated. The proceedings were greatly simplified by not having to take into account the opinion of the monophysites in Armenia, Egypt, and Syria, who were now all under Arab rule.

Victory over the Muslims did not bring lasting peace to the empire. The emperor Justinian II (685–95, restored 705–11) lost Armenia to the Arabs, and his harsh justice and taxes at home led to rising unpopularity. With the help of the Blues, a soldier named Leontios took power. Justinian II's nose was cut off and his tongue was slit in front of a crowd at the Hippodrome. This retribution was a common practice. Tradition did not allow a mutilated man to be emperor. To the Byzantines, the face was highly symbolic. Religious icons and secular art emphasized the face. The emperor was supposed to be God's agent on Earth, so mutilating his face would make him an imperfect vessel from which to exert God's will. Because cutting off the nose was rarely fatal, it effectively got rid of a rival while sparing his life. The coup was quick, but it led to thirty years of internal instability and a series of setbacks.

---

6. Norwich, *Short History of Byzantium*, p. 102.

IV.

INSTABILITY AND INVASION
(695–912)

The Byzantines would have been wise to keep Justinian II. After his fall, the Blues and Greens fought for control. The candidate for the Blues took the throne first, but was deposed three years later by someone supported by the Greens. Neither ruler could stop the Arabs. More territory was lost, including Carthage, the principal city of North Africa, in modern Tunisia.

Meanwhile Justinian II traveled the lands on the fringe of the empire looking for allies. He paid a visit to the Khazars, a seminomadic tribe north of the Black Sea, and married their chieftain's daughter. But the Khazar chief was tempted by the rich reward on the deposed emperor's head and tried to kidnap him. Justinian II heard of the plot in time and ambushed the two men sent to capture him, strangling them with his bare hands. Then he fled to the Bulgars. There he had better luck. The Bulgar khan agreed to help him regain his throne in return for the title of Caesar. Byzantium had the luster of being the new Rome, and foreign kings and chieftains always wanted Roman titles to increase their prestige.

By 705 he was back, with an army of Bulgars and Slavs behind him. They could not, of course, attack the walls directly, but Justinian II and some of his men crept into town through an old, dry water conduit. They overpowered the guards and opened the gates. The walls of Theodosius failed to protect the city only three times in more than a thousand years. That the first time would be to a Byzantine emperor seems somehow appropriate.

Justinian II was deeply changed by his ordeal. He had been publicly mutilated, exiled, and hunted like an animal for ten years. Now he took his revenge. Anyone who might have a claim to the throne was put to death. Some were tied up in bags and thrown into the sea. Others had their throats slit before cheering crowds in the Hippodrome. Others were hanged from the city walls. Through it all Justinian II watched, his terrible injury hidden by a false nose of pure gold.

He was a terror to his subjects, but he was still a capable leader. There were no serious defeats during his second reign, and he was able to reconcile with the pope, who came all the way to Constantinople to hammer out a compromise on the finer points of doctrine. The city would not see another Roman pope until 1967.

His success was not to last. There were a few political enemies he hadn't been able to track down. In 711, they took their vengeance and assassinated him. They put in his place an ineffectual man who spent most of his time hosting elegant parties, and was overthrown in his turn nineteen months later. This time, the rebels blinded the deposed emperor instead of merely cutting off his nose. Justinian II had proven that a mutilated man could still rule, so after him all deposed emperors were either blinded or killed outright.

Bronze belt buckle, sixth century or later. The larger medallion shows a bust of Christ.
SOURCE: Museum of Art and Archaeology, University of Missouri-Columbia.

The next emperor was made of sterner stuff and prepared for an all-out war against the Arabs. He marched east at the head of an immense army, but as soon as he was out of sight of the capital some of the troops who had stayed home grabbed an obscure tax collector named Theodosios and made him emperor (715–17). None of the soldiers wanted the job for themselves; it was too risky. Considering the life expectancy of emperors during this period, it is no surprise that their candidate became known as "Theodosios the Reluctant." While his so-called supporters were marching on the palace, he slipped away and had to be hunted down and dragged back to take his place on the throne. The nervous bureaucrat didn't last long in power and was happy to spend the rest of his life as a monk in return for not resisting the man who deposed him. Theodosios retired to a monastery, where he became a renowned holy man. His tomb became a shrine famed for its miracles. The reluctant emperor is now known as St. Theodosios in the Orthodox Church.

By this time Byzantium was in desperate need of stability. The Bulgars were making raids again (the peace treaty they had signed with Justinian II died with him) and the Arab threat still loomed on the horizon. What was needed was leadership.

Leo III (717–41), a former peasant turned general who easily took power from Theodosios the Reluctant in 717, arrived just in time. The Arabs attacked that same year. An army of 120,000 Muslim warriors surrounded the capital, and a fleet of eighteen hundred ships appeared on the Sea of Marmora. It was the largest force Constantinople had ever faced. Fortunately for the city, one of the previous emperors had taken time out from fighting his rivals to strengthen the walls and stock up on food. The Arabs found that they could not storm the massive land walls, and any time their ships tried to sail into the harbor of the Golden Horn, they were incinerated by Greek fire. They settled in for a long siege, hoping to starve the city into submission.

The winter that year was the worst in living memory, and soon the Arabs were freezing to death in cold, damp conditions they had never before experienced. They picked the land clean of food, and soon resorted to eating their mounts. When those were gone, some forced themselves to eat the bodies of their dead comrades. The Arabs flung themselves against the walls in desperation, urged on by the tempting smells wafting out of the city bakeries as they fired up their ovens every morning. The harsh weather buckled the hulls of the invaders' ships, and they started to leak.

By the following spring, the Arabs were desperate. Half their army was dead and the rest were barely able to fight. Then the Bulgars appeared. It is unclear whether they came to help the Byzantines or take Constantinople for themselves, but they finished what the Greeks and the winter had started. They slaughtered the Arabs and stripped the bodies of valuables. The few Arabs left alive fled back to their own territory. The fleet followed them, now reduced to only five ships. It was the worst defeat in the eighty-year campaign of Islamic conquest. Neither side would forget this battle.

The Bulgars surveyed the scene. To one side was the Arab camp, littered with mass graves and half-eaten corpses. To the other were the massive city walls, unharmed by a year's siege and mounted with strange devices that spouted fire no amount of water could quench. If they had come with the idea of taking Constantinople, they soon changed their minds. The Bulgar generals quietly gathered up their men and left.

The Byzantines did not see another Muslim army for a long time. In 750, the Caliphate shifted from the Syrian city of Damascus east to the Mesopotamian city of Baghdad, in modern Iraq. The caliphs were recognized by most Muslims as Muhammad's successors and leaders of the Islamic world. Like the Byzantine emperors, this honor brought with it both advantages and severe limitations. Failure was not acceptable, and the Ummayads in Syria had become weak. Their dynasty fell apart, but the Abbasid dynasty of Iraq took over leadership of the Muslim world. The focus of Islamic conquest shifted east. Baghdad replaced Damascus as the center of Islamic culture. The tide that washed against the walls of Constantinople would soon inundate eastern Persia and Afghanistan.

Leo III soundly defeated Byzantium's enemies, but what he did next turned the empire against itself. For many years the cult of the icons had increased in popularity. Icons were paintings of religious

Silver armband engraved with scenes from the life of Christ, sixth to seventh century. The inscription includes the first words of Psalm 91, "He who dwells in the shelter of the Most High will rest in the shadow of the Almighty."
SOURCE: Museum of Art and Archaeology, University of Missouri-Columbia.

figures, especially Jesus and the Virgin Mary, and were considered to be holy objects. They were prayed to for cures, were carried into battle, and were witnesses at legal proceedings just as portraits of the imperial family used to be in Diocletian's day. To Leo and other conservative Christians, this idolatry was a violation of the Second Commandment, which forbade the worship of graven images. Sculpture was never popular in Byzantium for this very reason. Iconoclasts ("image-breakers") considered the fact that icons were painted and not graven to be irrelevant. The spirit of the commandment was what mattered, not the letter.

The iconoclasts may have been influenced by the Arabs. Despite the frequent wars, Byzantium kept close economic ties with its neighbors. Between the battles there was a free flow of goods and ideas. This trade reached across much of the world. From China came the secret of making silk; from India came rare spices; from East Africa

Coptic tapestry showing a horseman brandishing a double axe. The various parts were woven out of wool and linen, then stitched together at a later date. The central panel dates to the sixth century, while the border dates to the eighth or ninth century. Coptic textiles were very colorful and were used for both clothing and decoration. Dealers, both ancient and modern, commonly sewed pieces of several textiles together to make large tapestries.

SOURCE: The Malcove Collection, University of Toronto Art Centre, Toronto, Canada.

came exotic animals; and from all of these places came ideas. Islam, like Leo's Christianity, also follows the Ten Commandments and takes the banning of all images very seriously, to the point that in most periods of Muslim history, no pictures of any living creatures were allowed. (In the early twentieth century, a Muslim religious leader ruled that photography was permitted, since a photograph is actually the preservation of a reflection, and nowhere in either the Bible or the Koran is there a rule against mirrors).

Also, Leo was from Syria, a region that had always fostered a stricter brand of Christianity. But there was another reason for banning the images. Icons were produced in monasteries. These institutions became very wealthy and influential from the sale of icons and through the generous donations of the faithful. Many Byzantines left land or money to local monasteries in their wills, believing that such bequests would increase one's chances of getting into Heaven. The accumulation of such donations over the years meant that the monasteries now controlled vast estates and the political power that came with them.

Leo decided to destroy all religious images in the empire, starting with a popular icon of Christ that hung above the gate to his palace. When a soldier tried to take it down, a group of nuns pulled the ladder out from underneath him. Leo had the nuns executed. Soon the people were honoring them as martyrs. But Leo pressed on, and this once-popular ruler alienated the pope and most of the Byzantine population.

His son Constantine V (741–75) inherited the problem when he came to the throne in 741. He was briefly deposed by an iconodule ("image-loving") rebel, but he retook his throne and tried to get rid of images once and for all. Anyone who was caught hiding or venerating icons was whipped or even killed. Thousands of monks, nuns, and regular citizens suffered for their beliefs at the hands of fellow Christians. Countless works of art were cut to pieces or thrown into bonfires. To reduce the size of religious institutions, he forced many monks and nuns to marry.

While Leo and his son Constantine warded off the Islamic threat and inflicted several defeats on the Bulgars, their clash with the

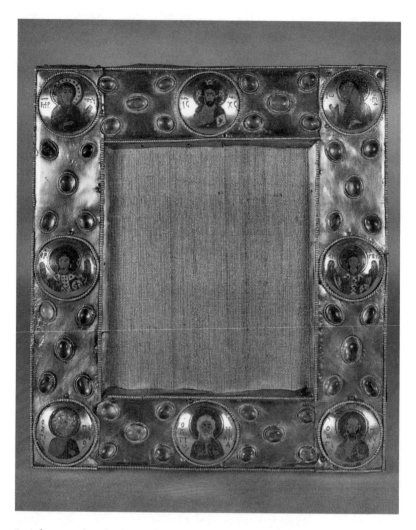

Icon frame with eight cloisonné medallions, eleventh century. Icons were venerated as holy objects, so they often were provided with rich frames. Sometimes the frames included hollow spaces to hold relics, although this one does not.

Ivory plaque with Nativity, Syro-Palestinian, seventh or eighth century.
SOURCE: Dumbarton Oaks, Byzantine Photograph and Fieldwork Archives, Washington, DC.

iconodule pope led to the loss of Italy. The Lombards, who had started out as just another Germanic tribe but had risen to become the greatest power in Italy, now tried to take over the entire region. They captured the imperial stronghold of Ravenna in 751.

The pope wanted protection against the Lombards, but he could no longer bring himself to make an alliance with the Byzantines, whom he saw as heretics under the rule of an emperor who thought he had greater say over religious affairs than the chosen representative of God in Rome. Instead he found an ally in the Franks, a Germanic tribe that had settled down to found a kingdom in what is now France and Germany. They became Rome's main supporters. The Frankish kings made an alliance with the pope, thereby becoming the most important of the emerging Germanic states. The Christians of the east and the Christians of the west would drift ever further apart.

When Leo IV (775–80) inherited the throne, the laws against the images were relaxed and the persecutions stopped. The new emperor, however, was a sickly man and soon died, leaving his wife Irene as regent over their underage son. Irene was devoted to icons; she slept with one under her pillow. She carried on her late husband's policies and began to depose or isolate all the iconoclast leaders in the Church and bureaucracy.

Her son, however, was an iconoclast, and he was coming of age. A power struggle ensued and Irene got the upper hand. She had the young man put in chains and ordered his eyes to be plucked out. She specifically instructed that the knife be pressed deep enough to cause internal bleeding. He died soon after, and Irene was in undisputed control.

Irene made a lot of enemies during her short reign (797–802). She was the first woman in Byzantine history to reign alone. Her solo sovereignty ruffled many traditionalists. The empress went so far as to sign her name "Irene, the Faithful Emperor," but the epithet did not help. Her treatment of her son was cruel even by Byzantine standards, and the people had many other reasons to want to be rid of her. The iconoclasts hated her for bringing back the images, and the army hated her for giving the Abbasid caliph in Baghdad tribute instead of going to war. But her downfall came from events occurring hundreds of miles to the west in Rome.

In the year 800 the pope proclaimed Charlemagne, the king of the Franks, as the new emperor of the Romans. The pope said that since there wasn't a man on the Byzantine throne the post was vacant. The Frankish kingdom became the new Rome. One of Charlemagne's first acts as emperor was to send a delegation to Constantinople to ask for Irene's hand in marriage. Irene appeared to approve of the idea. An alliance would secure her position and could make Justinian's old dream of a reunified Roman Empire a reality.

The people of Constantinople had had enough. For an upstart emperor, and a barbarian at that, to claim the Roman throne was completely unacceptable. The Byzantines saw the pope's move exactly for what it was—a snub to the Greeks. The pope wanted an emperor who would recognize his authority, and he knew he would never get that from a Byzantine ruler. To the Byzantines, Constantinople was the new Rome, not the ugly provincial town of Aachen that Charlemagne called his "capital." By 802, Irene was overthrown and there was a new emperor on the throne.

Nikephoros (802–11) wasted no time in fixing the situation. Irene had bankrupted the empire by constantly reducing taxes in a vain attempt at popularity. Nikephoros was the chief finance minister during her reign and felt it as a personal affront that he had to do a bad job in order to please his empress. Now he raised taxes for nearly everyone. He especially picked on the powerful monasteries. Nikephoros taxed them into submission.

He also cut off tribute to the Abbasid caliph in Baghdad. This refusal led to war, of course, but the conflict soon ground to a stalemate. Nikephoros was more worried about the Bulgars, who had developed a powerful empire of their own and were beginning to hold sway over the large Slav population in Greece. In 811, Nikephoros attacked.

At first all went well. The Byzantines torched the Bulgar capital at Pliska, but as they marched north they went through a narrow gorge in the Balkan Mountains and straight into a trap. The Bulgars rained arrows and spears down on the helpless Byzantines and set off a massive landslide that buried whole divisions of the army. Nikephoros was killed, and his son and heir Stavrakios was carried to Constantinople with a broken back. Krum, khan of the Bulgars, celebrated by having Nikephoros' skull plated with silver. He used it as a drinking cup and would often serve wine to Byzantine ambassadors in it.

Stavrakios was paralyzed and in immense pain. He tried to rule but was overthrown by his brother-in-law Michael I (811–13) after a month. Stavrakios was sent to a monastery, where he died after five months. Michael himself was overthrown after another humiliating defeat by the Bulgars. Leo V (813–20), known as "the Armenian," now took power. Soon Constantinople was enduring one of its frequent sieges. Leo offered terms to the Bulgars and called for a meeting with Khan Krum. When the Bulgar showed up, Leo V's soldiers tried to ambush him. Krum leapt onto his horse and sped away, dodging the javelins tossed after him. Krum was furious. The fact that he couldn't storm the Theodosian walls didn't help his mood. He took out his anger on the suburbs that lay outside the walls. Then Leo counterattacked, driving deep into Bulgar territory. While Krum stayed in Byzantine territory slaughtering Greek civilians, Leo marched through

Bulgaria slaughtering Bulgar civilians. The killing only stopped when Khan Krum unexpectedly died of a seizure.

His successor, Khan Omurtag, made a peace treaty with Leo. The two met personally; this time there was no trickery. To seal the deal, the pagan Bulgar placed his hand on a Bible and swore to uphold the treaty. Leo made the oath in the Bulgar way—on a pile of dead dogs topped by a sword.

Leo had proved his worth. The previous three emperors had been iconodules and had brought disaster to the empire. The Byzantines began to believe that the images really were a sin and were bringing the wrath of God down upon the empire. Iconoclasm was on the rise again, and Leo was quick to ride the wave. In 814, images were banned once more.

This decree brought him popularity, but it did not keep him from being assassinated by an ambitious officer named Michael II (820–29), whose reign was disrupted by civil wars and Arab raids. The Arabs took Crete and used it as a base for pirate attacks until the Byzantines retook it in 961. Michael II did accomplish two important things—he established a new dynasty and was able to secure a peaceful transfer of power to his son Theophilos. Michael II died of natural causes, a rare accomplishment for emperors of this period.

The empire needed a ruler like Theophilos (829–42). He was a lavish spender and builder like Justinian. He strengthened Constantinople's defenses and greatly expanded the imperial palace. One of his additions to the throne room was a remarkable invention, a description of which would sound like an anachronism if it didn't come from the pen of a contemporary observer.

The throne was positioned under a golden tree. On the branches were jewel-encrusted birds. When a foreign visitor was ushered into the emperor's presence the birds began to sing and hopped onto the throne. After singing for a time, they would stop and the audience would begin. The conversation ended when the birds began to sing again. Sometimes, in order to impress a more sophisticated observer, the entire throne—emperor, tree and all—would rise up into the ceiling, then lower back down, the emperor having mysteriously changed his clothes in the meantime.

This device was nothing other than the world's first robot. Steam driven, in all likelihood, and capable of only the simplest of tasks, but a mechanism of a complexity not seen until the automatons of the nineteenth century.

Despite his ornate ways, which delighted his countrymen and astonished foreign delegates, Theophilos was one of the most approachable emperors. On Sundays he would ride from his palace to a church on the other side of town while his subjects followed along and talked with him. He would also slip from his palace at night dressed as a commoner to mingle with the people and hear their real opinions.

His combination of regal mannerisms and humanity made him popular enough to get away with reintroducing iconoclasm. He was milder than previous iconoclastic emperors; few monks and painters suffered under his reign. When he died in 842 he was succeeded by his son Michael III (842–67), who was only three years old at the time. The boy's mother, Theophilos' widow Theodora, ruled for him. She declared that the palace no longer opposed the veneration of images, and thousands of icons miraculously appeared from their hiding places. The sheer amount of preserved images, and the fair number of works painted during the iconoclastic period, showed just how little the population heeded the law.

Michael III did not grow up to be a particularly religious man; his favorite pastime was going on drunken binges during which he and his friends terrorized the capital, but he spread Christianity further than any other emperor. His first converts were in Moravia, a Slavic kingdom in what is now Hungary. The Moravians were worried that their enemies the Bulgars, who had recently signed a treaty with the Franks, might convert to Catholicism. The Moravian aristocracy saw no choice but to convert to Orthodoxy so they could align themselves with the Byzantines.

Michael III sent two monks named Cyril and Methodius to teach them Christianity. Cyril was a brilliant linguist, and while in the Slavic lands was able to preach in the local language. During his mission Cyril invented an alphabet called Glagolitic to match the sounds of the Moravian language so that the illiterate converts could read and write their language for the first time. Cyril soon translated the Bible so they would have something to read. Their followers later adapted the Greek alphabet to produce Cyrillic, which is still used by most Slavic speakers to this day.

Attempts were made to woo the Bulgars as well, but they were not impressed when they found that the Orthodox missionaries were constantly arguing among themselves over obscure points of doctrine. The khan made repeated appeals to Constantinople for clarification, but was met with either curt replies or silence. Rome, however, offered a unified doctrine. Although the khan himself had been baptized in a grand Orthodox ceremony at the Hagia Sophia, he allowed his subjects to become Catholics.

Michael III's successor was Basil (867–86), a former stable boy who curried the emperor's favor with his ability to train horses and his good company during Michael's parties. Basil proved to be very helpful indeed. When Michael wanted to bring his mistress into the palace under the eye of the empress, he had Basil marry her. The "couple" had a son who eventually became emperor, but it is not known if he was Basil's son or Michael's. But this strange arrangement didn't lead to the two falling out; Michael's descent into alcoholism did. Michael had become useless as a ruler, and Basil saw his chance. He invited the emperor to a party, waited until he was nearly passed out from drinking, then had his followers stab Michael to death. Basil was already ruling in all but name, so the transition of power was quick and undisputed.

Now the Bulgars sent a legation to Constantinople. The Roman missionaries, it turned out, were grasping, intolerant, and unpopular. Rome denied the Bulgars their own patriarchate, and when the offer was not forthcoming from Basil, the khan asked if Bulgaria should be under the jurisdiction of Rome or Constantinople. Basil called a council of the five patriarchs—Jerusalem, Alexandria, Antioch, Rome, and Constantinople. Not surprisingly, the majority voted for Constantinople. Bulgaria became, and continues to be, part of the Orthodox Church.

As Orthodox Christianity spread through the Slavic lands, Islam spread eastwards into what are now the Central Asian Republics. The

Apse mosaic of the Virgin and Child, Hagia Sophia, Constantinople. A nearby inscription states "The images which the imposters had cast down here pious emperors have again set up." This seems to be a reference to Michael III (842–67) and Basil I (867–86), who reinstated icons and other religious images after the iconoclastic controversy.

Islamic empire had broken up into several different caliphates that fought each other as much as they did the infidel. The Muslims were still an important power, and most of the Byzantine army remained on the eastern frontier, but they no longer threatened the Byzantines with extinction.

Basil's (or Michael's) son was Leo VI (886–912). He came into power in a rather unusual way. Perhaps because of his questionable legitimacy, Basil never liked Leo. He even threw him in prison for a short time. He named another of his sons as successor, but the young man died. Basil was so wracked with grief that he had his dead son canonized. This preferential treatment did nothing to improve Leo's opinion of his "father." That Basil came to a bad end is not surprising.

The official story was that Basil was out hunting, his favorite pastime, when a stag he was chasing unexpectedly turned on him. The stag rammed him and managed to hook one of his antlers under the emperor's belt. He was pulled from his horse and, we are told, dragged sixteen miles. Amazingly, the seventy-four-year-old Basil survived long enough to have the distance measured and recorded for posterity. This story is the only version that has come down to us. While it is so obviously false, there is no definite proof that Leo murdered him.

Leo's behavior would continue to raise eyebrows in Constantinople. He didn't love his first wife, and soon started an affair. When his first wife died, having borne him only a daughter, he married his mistress. But she also died without producing an heir. Byzantine law and Orthodox tradition forbade third marriages, but Leo got special permission from the patriarch to take a new wife. She was soon pregnant, but tragedy again struck the hapless emperor. She died in childbirth, and the baby, the long hoped-for son, also died. Leo took another mistress. This time the woman was able to give birth to a living son.

Leo was determined to make the boy his heir. Knowing that the patriarch would never allow a fourth marriage, the couple married in secret. When the patriarch found out, he was enraged and excommunicated the emperor. Leo simply deposed him and brought in a more tractable man for the job. He also obtained a letter from the pope declaring the fourth marriage legal. Such disregard for religious sensibilities did little to endear him to his people, but they would soon regret his passing.

This mosaic in the Hagia Sophia in Constantinople shows an emperor kneeling in supplication before Christ. It is generally believed to show Leo VI (886–912) begging forgiveness for his unsanctioned fourth marriage. Significantly, this image appears above the door through which the emperor had to enter to attend mass.

SOURCE: Dumbarton Oaks, Byzantine Photograph and Fieldwork Archives, Washington, DC.

Mosaic of the emperor Alexander (912–13) in the Hagia Sophia, Constantinople. Alexander is identified by the monograms around him. He is dressed in ceremonial regalia.

V.

VICTORY AND DISASTER

(912–1071)

Although Leo was unlucky in love, he was an able and fair ruler. Unfortunately for the Byzantines, he was succeeded by his drunkard brother Alexander (912–13). Alexander spent much of his time at parties. He developed a besotted attachment to a statue of a boar in the Hippodrome, coming to believe that it was the embodiment of his soul. When a Bulgarian envoy showed up to renew the peace treaty his brother had signed, he flew into a rage and, rising unsteadily from his throne, told them that there would be no treaty. Seeing what kind of man they were dealing with, the envoys left, plotting an invasion.

Before they could act, Alexander died, apparently while sacrificing to the boar in an attempt to cure his impotence. His successor, Constantine VII (913–59), was not yet of age and was dominated by the same shadowy figures who had ruled the empire while Alexander was in his cups. The Bulgarians showed up and encircled the city. Realizing as so many others had before them that they could not storm the walls, the khan struck a deal. The tribute Leo had paid during his reign would be reinstated, and Constantine would marry one of the khan's daughters, thus bringing the Bulgarians into the imperial succession. In return, there would be peace and Bulgaria would stay within the Orthodox Church.

But the khan's hopes were dashed by Constantine's mother Zoe. Many in the court were uneasy with the idea of a potential Bulgarian emperor, so she was able to garner a great deal of support. She rescinded the deal and, predictably, the Bulgarians marched on Constantinople again. This time they annihilated two Byzantine armies sent to stop them. While the power struggle in the palace kept the political factions occupied, the Bulgarians looted the countryside.

Eventually the Bulgarians left, laden with booty. The Bulgarian Orthodox Church declared its independence. The Byzantines would not regain their influence over the Bulgars for many years to come.

In the fight for the throne, Constantine VII managed to struggle to the top. He sent the other claimants to monasteries and took full control. By all accounts he was an effective and just ruler. He patronized the arts (he was an accomplished painter himself) and began to rebuild the provinces after so many years of warfare and internal conflict. The khan of Bulgaria was busy putting down civil wars. The caliphates were similarly divided. For these reasons, Byzantium experienced one of its rare periods of peace.

Constantine used this breathing space to confiscate land from the rural aristocracy and redistribute it to the peasants. Perhaps he was motivated by personal reasons, as most of his rivals had been from the rural elite, but the move made good practical sense as well. Small landholders had never been a political force. Many of them were soldiers in the theme system, and they were more easily controlled. Each theme was run by a strategos (general), and the soldiers got portions of it to farm. Their land came with their job, and the emperor controlled both. The owners of large estates, on the other hand, were a political force that Constantine needed to hold in check. When he died in 959 he left the empire, both its common people and culture, immeasurably richer.

His son Romanos II (959–63) now took the throne. He proved to be as able as his father. Byzantium had no aggressive enemies, so the time was ripe for expansion. Romanos sent the brilliant general Nikephoros Phokas (whose first name means "Bringer of Victory") with a huge fleet and fifty thousand men to Crete, which for many years had been the base for Muslim pirates who terrorized the eastern

Bronze reliquary cross from the tenth century. This cross opened up to show a relic of Christ or one of the saints, now lost. Reliquaries like these were treasured possessions of churches and noblemen.

SOURCE: Museum of Art and Archaeology, University of Missouri-Columbia.

Mediterranean. After a hard winter's fighting, the Byzantines took the island but soon had to hurry back home. An Arab raiding party had entered Byzantine territory. The Byzantines ambushed the Arabs in a mountain pass, crushing almost the entire army in an artificial landslide. Then they marched all the way to Aleppo in Syria. They were not able to hold much of the land they captured, but the campaign had an incredible effect on morale. For the first time in far too long, the Byzantines were on the offensive.

Nikephoros Phokas rode into Constantinople to an ecstatic welcome, holding aloft the tunic of John the Baptist, part of the plunder from Aleppo. He had returned at the urging of the empress Theophano. Romanos II had died, leaving his eunuch minister Bringas in charge of state affairs. Theophano was regent over her two young sons, but she feared a coup before they came of age. The general was her only hope. Between them they orchestrated a coup against Bringas, while the army proclaimed the popular general as the new emperor.

Phokas was a cunning general, but he did not inspire loyalty. A religious fanatic, he spent most of his waking hours in church. At night he would sleep on the ground in a hair shirt, a rough garment of bristly hide with the hair turned inward. This was the favored dress of religious ascetics because it was itchy, uncomfortable, and usually foul-smelling. His choice of fashion did nothing to improve his nasty temperament.

Despite his personality, and his vow of chastity, Phokas married the empress. The woman had little choice; marriage to Phokas was better than blinding or imprisonment in a nunnery. For Phokas the marriage was a sound political move; it gave him legitimacy. While his place on the throne was debatable, hers was unquestioned.

Now that his position was secure, Phokas resumed his war on the Muslims. He retook Cyprus, a victory that helped bring down the Abbasid caliphate in Baghdad. The resulting internal strife among the Muslims would keep the eastern border secure for many years.

But Phokas was a better general than diplomat. When Bulgarian envoys showed up for their annual tribute, he had them tortured and sent back empty-handed. Then he raided their country. He didn't

The Hosios Loukas Monastery in Phokis, Greece. The first church was built in the tenth century by a general who used to consult with the religious hermit Loukas at the site, and rebuilt by Romanos II (959–63). The second, smaller church on the right was built in the early eleventh century.

SOURCE: School of Architecture, College of Architecture, Planning, and Landscape Architecture, University of Arizona.

have enough troops available to win the decisive victory he wanted, so he hired the prince of Kiev to help. Kiev was the capital of the Rus, Viking settlers who had left Scandinavia to colonize Russia. Kiev was the greatest of the Russian kingdoms and would not be superceded by Moscow until the fourteenth century. The Rus soon controlled the river trade leading from the Russian heartland to the Black Sea. Their merchants and rulers got rich trading furs, amber, honey, wax, and slaves for the silks and other manufactured goods of Constantinople.

The prince of Kiev was happy to get involved in Balkan politics. He took much of Bulgaria for himself and then demanded the same tribute the Bulgars wanted. Phokas had simply replaced one tribute for another, and a weak neighbor for a strong one.

Phokas also reversed earlier land reforms and allowed the rural aristocracy to start buying out the peasants. He raised taxes, so that working people had no choice but to borrow from the rich and, when they defaulted, to lose their land. The disparity in wealth this tax increase caused made him increasingly unpopular. The empress Theophano took a lover, a handsome Armenian soldier named John Tzimiskes, and together they plotted the emperor's downfall. One snowy night in the middle of winter, John and some of his followers crept into Phokas' room, took turns beating him, and then cut off his head. But Theophano was betrayed by the man she trusted. John sent her off to a nunnery as soon as he took power.

Although he had no legitimate right to the throne, John (969–76) soon became a popular ruler. He distributed most of his personal fortune to the poor. He also launched a full-scale invasion of Bulgaria in an effort to push out the remaining troops of the prince of Kiev. He defeated the Russian army, thus effectively neutralizing his predecessor's mistake, then fought the Bulgars.

The campaign went well and soon the Byzantines were besieging the Bulgarian capital, Preslav. The defenders cowered inside as John's troops used catapults to launch Greek fire over the city walls. The unquenchable fire proved to be just as effective on land as it was at sea. The fire spread quickly and the Bulgars were forced to surrender. Southern Bulgaria became a Byzantine province once more. John's eastern campaign was equally successful. Soon he ruled over much of Syria and Mesopotamia, lost three hundred years before in the initial Arab onslaught.

Bulgaria would not be fully taken until the long reign of Basil II (976–1025), known to history and his contemporaries as "Basil the Bulgar-Slayer." The title was well earned. When Basil came to power after John died, the Bulgars were not entirely beaten. From their enclaves in the north they gathered under their leader Samuel, now called "Tsar" instead of "Khan" in imitation of the powerful Russian rulers. The change had come under the mighty Simeon the Great (893–923), one of the most effective rulers in Bulgarian history. Simeon chose this title because it was the Slavic version of "Caesar." The Bulgars had long since left behind their nomadic ways and created a strong and highly cultured empire of their own, so Simeon and later rulers felt they deserved the title.

Basil was determined to stop the Bulgars from reestablishing their empire, but he had problems at home that had to be dealt with first. A number of aristocrats from Asia Minor were trying to seize the throne, and for the first decade of his reign he was in almost constant danger of assassination. To secure his position he turned to an unlikely ally—Vladimir of Kiev.

Vladimir was a pagan, but he was dissatisfied with his religion and was looking for a new one. The clergy sent by the Catholics, Muslims, and Jews failed to impress him. However, his ambassadors attended a service held at the Hagia Sophia in his honor and reported that it was so beautiful that they felt they had risen to Heaven. Vladimir offered to convert in exchange for the hand of Basil's sister Anna in marriage. The woman was sent to Kiev, along with an entourage of Orthodox clergy who set about converting Vladimir's subjects. For the first time, a member of the Byzantine royal family married a pagan foreigner. Today, Russia remains one of the most important regions of the Orthodox Church.

In gratitude Vladimir sent six thousand Viking warriors, huge men wielding fearsome battle-axes. With this help, Basil's domestic problems were over. The Vikings stayed and became the emperor's personal bodyguard, known as the Varangian Guard. While they were the emperor's loyal protectors, they never fully converted to Byzantine ways. Many remained pagans. To idle away time during the long Orthodox masses they had to endure in the Hagia Sophia, they carved their names in Viking runes into the marble banisters and columns. An observant visitor can still find them.

Basil now was free to deal with the Bulgars, who were making repeated raids into Byzantine territory. He marched out to stop them, but his army was ambushed in 989 and cut to pieces. Basil barely made it back to Constantinople alive. Shortly afterwards, a severe earthquake destroyed or damaged dozens of churches in Constantinople. A great crack appeared in the dome of the Hagia Sophia. It didn't collapse, but the damage was enough of an omen to make the Byzantines wonder why God was angry with them.

Leaf from a Gospel book, eleventh or early twelfth century. The evangelist Matthew is shown sitting at a lectern writing on a scroll. This image was a popular one in the empire, because it combined the love of Christianity and the love of learning, both central to Byzantine thought. This example is painted on parchment, an animal skin, usually of sheep or goat, treated and used for books. Vellum, which was made from the skin of a calf, was of better quality but more expensive.
SOURCE: The Malcove Collection, University of Toronto Art Centre, Toronto Canada.

Something needed to be done to improve morale. Basil assembled a large army and, after some rigorous training, marched into Bulgaria. He moved cautiously, keeping the troops together and avoiding any place that might make a good ambush spot. He didn't get far. News came that the Arabs had Aleppo surrounded. Basil was frustrated. Aleppo was an important city and had to be saved, but it was hundreds of miles away in Syria. The enemy he most despised was waiting for him in Bulgaria, but the other threat could not be ignored. The advance stopped.

Basil rushed back to the capital and gathered another army. To increase his speed, he had the entire force mounted, something that had never been done with a Byzantine army before. The Byzantine army, like the Roman army before it, was mostly infantry. Campaigns were slow because the troops had to walk to the battlefield, a daunting task when the battlefield was half an empire away. Basil bought each of his men two mules and hurried to Aleppo in just sixteen days, almost as fast as the imperial mail service.

The Arabs were caught completely by surprise. They thought the Byzantines were at least a month away. Victory was easy for Basil, and he lost no time riding back to Bulgaria again. On his way back through Asia Minor, he was shocked to see how rich and powerful the local aristocracy had become. Vast estates boasted sumptuous mansions that rivaled anything in the capital. Their owners commanded private armies; some even minted their own currency. These mansions stood side by side with the miserable shacks of the subsistence farmers. Most of these poor families were in debt to their wealthy neighbors. When they couldn't pay, they found their little farms absorbed into the larger estates. The land reforms of Constantine VII had been reversed by less conscientious emperors, and now the estates were as large as ever. Basil was furious. These were the noblemen who had led uprisings against him earlier in his reign. He was determined to break their power and growing independence.

He passed an edict nullifying any property transfers that didn't date back to the reign of Romanos I (920–44). If the land had been owned by someone else during that time, it was returned without compensation. Many of the rich families were ruined, while the poor celebrated a windfall.

Ivory rosette casket with warriors, Dionysiac figures and animals, Constantinople, tenth or eleventh century. Classical imagery never went out of style in Byzantium. Some of the figures here recall Roman images of the rites of Dionysus, also called Bacchus, the god of wine.

SOURCE: Dumbarton Oaks, Byzantine Photograph and Fieldwork Archives, Washington, DC.

The Bulgar tsar Samuel used the lull in Basil's campaign to move west and conquer the lands that now make up Bosnia. While this rural area had never been under firm Byzantine control, the towns on the Dalmatian coast were a rich source of tax revenue. Now they were all but cut off from the empire. Basil made a unique decision. He offered the towns to the doge of Venice, an Italian city-state that was just beginning to come into its own as a commercial trading power. The doge would rule them in the emperor's name. This deal was a bargain for both sides. Venice got its first colonies, and a position from which to attack the Croatian pirates who were terrorizing its shipping, while the Byzantines gained a powerful ally in Italy.

Now Basil was free to tackle the Bulgars. For the next fourteen years he worked his way up the Balkan Peninsula. Progress was slow and the Bulgars fought for every inch of ground, but the Byzantine advance was relentless. The war culminated in a fierce battle in 1014 during which the Bulgar army was scattered. Basil took fifteen thousand prisoners. He divided them into groups of one hundred, then had ninety-nine from each group blinded. From the hundredth man he took only one eye, so that he could lead his comrades back home. When these pitiful columns made it back to the tsar's capital, Samuel took one look at them and fell dead of a heart attack. The Bulgarian resistance continued for another four years, but now there was no doubt about the outcome.

Basil was one of the strongest emperors in Byzantium's eleven-hundred-year history, but he was a failure in one critical sense—he never married or produced an heir. If he had known what kind of men were to succeed him, he might have made having children a priority.

Instead, he was succeeded by his brother Constantine VIII (1025–28), a stylish, indolent man whose only good quality seems to have been that he was an excellent cook. When he wasn't inventing new sauces, or watching pornographic plays in his private theatre, he was gouging out the eyes of anyone he suspected of being an enemy. He would often be wracked with guilt afterwards, and beg forgiveness from his sightless victims. The man was obviously unstable, but Basil had so cowed the empire's enemies that there was little to fear on the international front. The Byzantine peasants, however, had a great deal to fear. While the emperor busied himself with his hobbies, the displaced rural aristocracy took the opportunity to snatch back their lands.

Constantine died, saving the empire from further embarrassment, and the throne devolved to his daughter Zoe. She married an aging senator named Romanos III Argyros, the mayor of Constantinople. Romanos was already married, but someone had to marry Zoe to keep the imperial line unbroken, and the court saw Romanos as the best candidate. Romanos' wife was sent off to a nunnery and the marriage went forward.

Unfortunately, Romanos II (1028–34) was in his sixties and was unable to impregnate his new wife. Zoe was frustrated (it never seemed to have occurred to the empress, who was already in her fifties, that she might be barren herself) and soon fell in love with a teenage courtier named Michael (1034–41). The two hatched a plot to poison the emperor. The poison didn't kill him immediately and Romanos, thinking he was ill, staggered into his bath to relax. Once he got in some of his attendants pressed his head underwater until he drowned. Zoe then married Michael after observing a period of mourning lasting several hours.

But ill health and epilepsy had made Michael impotent. He worried that his epilepsy was divine retribution for Romanos' murder. As a result, he spent most of his time in church praying for the salvation of his soul. He also brought beggars into the palace, personally caring for their needs. Michael's health deteriorated, but even though he was half dead he called up enough willpower to ride out to quell a rebellion in Bulgaria in 1040. He was so sick that he spent the night before the army's departure being treated by his physicians. Nevertheless, by morning he was atop a horse and leading his men into war as was expected of an emperor. He returned leading the rebel chief in chains, blinded and noseless. A year later, Michael died.

Power now passed into the hands of Michael and Zoe's adopted son Michael V Kalaphates (1041–42). The name means "ship's caulker," after his father's occupation; Michael was one of the many self-made men to make it to the Byzantine throne. The new emperor showed his gratitude by banishing the aging Zoe to a nunnery, inciting the people of Constantinople to riot. Michael Psellus, who worked as one of the emperor's secretaries and who wrote a detailed history of this period, described what happened next.

"As for the common mob, it was already on the move, greatly stirred at the prospect of exercising tyranny over him who had himself played the tyrant. And the women—but how can I explain this to people who did not know them? I myself saw some of them, whom nobody till then had seen outside the women's quarters, appearing in public and shouting and beating their breasts and lamenting terribly at the empress's misfortune. . . . Every man was armed; one clasped in his hands an axe, another brandished a heavy iron broadsword, another handled a bow, and another a spear, but the bulk of the mob, with some of the biggest stones in the folds of their clothing and holding others ready in their hands, ran in general disorder. . . . It was as if the whole multitude were sharing in some superhuman inspiration. They seemed changed persons. There was more madness in their running, more strength in their hands, the flash in their eyes was fiery and impassioned, the muscles in their bodies more powerful. As for prevailing on them to behave in a more dignified manner or dissuading them from their intentions, nobody whatever was willing to try such a thing."[1]

Michael had no choice but to bring the popular empress back. But that wasn't enough to appease the people. Soon, dissatisfaction with Michael spread to the palace guard and aristocracy. Michael was seen as a usurper by the common people, but the aristocracy saw him as a threat to their interests because of his reforms to curb their power. Led by the Viking hero Harold Hardrada, who later would become king of Norway, the palace guard grabbed the emperor and blinded him. Michael had ruled less than five months.

---

1. Psellus, "Chronographia," pp. 138–40. Reproduced by permission of Penguin Books, Ltd.

Zoe married a third time. Although she was bald at the wedding, owing to the Byzantine tradition of nuns shaving their heads, she at least got to marry someone she was attracted to for more than political reasons. Constantine IX (1042–55), was a man with whom she had been so friendly that her husband had become jealous and exiled him. Now Constantine was reinstated. Constantine was the worst of Zoe's choices in husbands. Profligate and heedless of the future, he reduced military spending so he could shower his favorites with expensive gifts. By 1055, both Constantine and Zoe had died. The only positive legacy this emperor would leave was to reinstate the University of Constantinople, leading to a revival of learning and the arts that had been sadly neglected by more pragmatic rulers such as Basil.

Since the death of Basil, Byzantium had seen a rapid succession of emperors. Zoe, while not much of a politician herself, at least provided some stability. The next twenty-five years saw six emperors, two empresses, and five civil wars. The bureaucracy, the landed aristocracy, and the army all vied for control, and factions within these factions caused even more turmoil. Fear of the army's power led some rulers to make deep cuts in military spending, a policy that would prove disastrous. To the Byzantines, it would become known as the "Time of Troubles." Psellus, who lived through this unhappy period, said,

> "Not one of the emperors in my time—and I say this with the experience of many in my life, for most of them only lasted a year—not one of them, to my knowledge, bore the burden of empire entirely free from blame *to the end*. Some were naturally evil, others were evil through their friendship for certain individuals, and others again for some other of the common reasons."[2]

In 1071, the Seljuk Turks invaded Byzantium from the east. A once-obscure Muslim tribe, they turned the Abbasid caliphate in

---

2. Psellus, "Chronographia," pp. 91–92. Reproduced by permission of Penguin Books, Ltd.

Mosaic of the Emperor Constantine IX (1042–55) and Zoe flanking Christ, Hagia Sophia, Constantinople. This scene shows the annual ceremony at which the emperor, shown here with a bag of coins, and the empress, shown here with a document, donated money and land to the church.

SOURCE: Dumbarton Oaks, Byzantine Photograph and Fieldwork Archives, Washington, DC.

Baghdad into a vassal state and took over Mesopotamia and Persia. The emperor at the time, Romanos IV, marched out to face them. The two armies met at the Armenian town of Manzikert. The Byzantines outnumbered the Turks, but the Greek general, Andronikos Doukas, spread a rumor during the battle that the Byzantines had already lost. Soon the emperor discovered that much of his army was retreating, and he and his few remaining men were surrounded. The emperor was captured while Andronikos hurried back to Constantinople to install his weak-willed and controllable stepson on the throne.

In the ensuing confusion the Turks marched through eastern Asia Minor, bringing their families and flocks with them. This influx of new people was worse than any of the Germanic or Slavic immigrations of previous centuries. Other tribes were happy to settle down and farm the land, and most eventually converted to Christianity and assimilated. But the Seljuk Turks had no interest in any of these things. A pastoral people, they had no use for cities and leveled any they captured. Their rather simplistic version of Islam urged them to slaughter Christians. Their vast flocks destroyed the farmland—they literally grazed it into desert. An anonymous chronicler tells of the province's ruin:

> ". . . almost the whole world, on land and sea, occupied by the impious barbarians, has been destroyed and has become empty of population, for all Christians have been slain by them and all houses and settlements with their churches have been devastated by them in the whole East, completely crushed and reduced to nothing."[3]

Asia Minor was almost entirely destroyed. Byzantium was forever weakened. But worse was yet to come.

---

3. Vasiliev, *History of the Byzantine Empire,* p. 355.

VI.

THE EMPIRE BETRAYED

(1071–1204)

The treachery of Andronikos at Manzikert led to the loss of most of Asia Minor, Byzantium's most productive province, and upset the carefully constructed theme system. The themes had worked well since their introduction in the seventh century. The government gave grants of land to the soldiers, and got loyal and permanent frontier forces in return. Most of the themes had been in Asia Minor, where the threat was great and the land plentiful. With this system in shambles, the empire was reduced to hiring expensive and unreliable foreign mercenaries. Never since the days of Diocletian had the Roman army seemed so alien to its people.

While the eastern part of Asia Minor was falling to the Seljuk Turks, a new threat came from the west. The Lombards, the Germanic tribe that controlled most of Italy, were using Norman mercenaries to defend their lands. The Normans were descendents of the Vikings who settled on the northern coast of France, a region that is still called Normandy. Unlike their distant cousins the Rus, the Normans were Catholics. Normandy was one of the many young nation-states appearing in western Europe.

The Lombards specifically hired Normans because they were more acculturated than many of the other Germanic tribes. The Normans, like the Lombards, were Catholics, understood Latin, and were used to centralized government. More importantly, their homeland

Panagia ton Chalkeon, south facade, Thessaloniki, 1149. Churches at this time tended to be smaller and made of brick. While this may have been a cost-saving measure after the loss of most of Asia Minor to the Seljuk Turks, Byzantine architects made the most of what they had and created attractive buildings.

<small>SOURCE:</small> Slobodan Curcic.

was sufficiently distant that they did not appear to be a threat, and they wouldn't have been if the Lombards had learned from their own history. But the Lombards paid the Normans with land, which was exactly what the Ostrogoths had done with the Lombards three hundred years before. The Lombards had used their new resources to overthrow the Ostrogoths. Now the Normans did the same to the Lombards. Soon the Normans were in control of much of the countryside. They sent for reinforcements from Normandy and by 1071 had overthrown the Lombards and pushed the Byzantines out of their last strongholds in Italy.

The Normans were expanding in northern Europe as well. In 1066 their king, thereafter known as William the Conqueror (known to the rest of Europe as William the Bastard), invaded England and defeated the Anglo-Saxon king Harold at the Battle of Hastings. William was soon the master of all England. The English almost won the battle, but they were tired after defeating a Viking force led by the Norwegian king Harold Hardrada, the former member of the Varangian guard who helped kill Michael V Kalaphates. He had tried to conquer England too, but all he accomplished was to give the Normans an easy victory.

The Normans ran an efficient and strict government in all their lands. Feudal lords, protected by well-built castles, kept the peace with brutal efficiency. While their culture and government were not as sophisticated as those of the Byzantines, they were able to summon up large and fearsome armies.

After consolidating their gains in Italy, the Normans sailed to Greece to attack Byzantium. The invasion came at a vulnerable time for the empire. The loss of eastern Asia Minor stripped Byzantium of half its population and its most productive farmland. Nevertheless, Emperor Alexios Komnenos (1081–1118) marched against them. At the forefront were the Varangian Guard, now mostly made up of Anglo-Saxon Englishmen who had fled their country after the defeat of King Harold. The Battle of Hastings was replayed in Greece, and once again the English lost. The Varangian Guard were surrounded and fought bravely, but by the end of the day they were wiped out. The rest of the Byzantine army retreated in disorder.

There followed a long and bloody war for the next four years. The Normans destroyed much of the Greek countryside. Venice came in on the side of the Greeks. They were one of the last holdouts in Italy and did not want their little city-state to be swallowed up by the Normans. Their help tipped the balance. The Norman advance stalled. It finally collapsed completely when a typhoid epidemic killed off most of the Norman army. This war was the first time Venetians and Byzantines fought side by side. The relationship between the aging empire of the Romans and the young, dynamic city-state would become ever closer over the centuries, to the infinite regret of the Greeks.

Alexios was a different sort of leader than Byzantium had seen for a long time. Brave, intelligent, and charismatic, he had a long and stable reign and founded a powerful dynasty that ruled for a hundred years. While he could not reverse the disaster at Manzikert, he revived the empire after the Time of Troubles and gave the people new hope.

The Normans were gone, but the Turks were still a problem. They controlled a large section of Byzantine territory, including most of the richest lands of Anatolia. Alexios appealed to Pope Urban II for help in pushing them out. But Urban had more ambitious plans. He called for a Crusade to free Byzantium and the Holy Land from the grip of the Muslims. He also promised that anyone who joined would be forgiven for all his past sins.

The popular reaction to Pope Urban's plea was astounding. In the previous four centuries, the Germanic tribes of western Europe had settled down into a patchwork of feudal states, where knights gave oaths of fealty to their lords, offering military support in exchange for land. The land came with peasants, who worked the fields and paid taxes. The peasants also had to farm the knight's fields for free, in exchange for protection. Inheritance was based on the rights of the firstborn son, so Europe was filled with younger sons of noblemen who had money, ambition, training, and no opportunities. They leapt at the chance to carve out estates for themselves in the wealthy eastern lands.

Commoners joined the Crusades as well. Life for the average peasant in medieval Europe was one of ceaseless toil. They often suffered abuse at the hands of the knights or lords to whom they were

Psalter and New Testament manuscript, showing St. Paul with his assistants St. Thecla and St. Timothy, Constantinople, ca. 1084. St. Thecla was miraculously saved from martyrdom twice, once when the pagans tried to burn her at the stake and again when they threw her to wild beasts. She was a popular saint with Byzantine women.

Squire and knight in the First Crusade

Nineteenth-century rendering of Crusaders.

SOURCE: *Historic Costume in Pictures*, by Braun & Schneider (Dover Publications, Inc., 1975).

bound. Many peasants were not even allowed to travel without their lord's permission. Soon, thousands of peasants were fleeing their farms in hopes of finding a better life in the Holy Land. The first wave of Crusaders arrived in Byzantium in 1097 under the leadership of an unkempt French monk named Peter the Hermit. The Crusaders were mostly French and German peasants fresh from looting and burning their way across Hungary. They came to Constantinople and began robbing its inhabitants in the name of the Crusade. The pope told them they were on a holy quest and that their sins were forgiven, so the uneducated farmers took that to mean they were free to do as they pleased. Alexios shipped them across the Bosphorus to Asia Minor as quickly as he could, where the Turks immediately massacred them.

The next Crusader armies arrived shortly thereafter. They were composed of trained knights and soldiers from all across Europe and were better behaved and far better organized. That worried Alexios even more. He could have handled Peter the Hermit's peasant rabble almost as easily as the Turks did, but these new forces posed a significant threat. He put them under escort and was careful to keep them happy with food and a steady supply of gifts. He managed to get oaths of fealty from most of the leadership. The Crusader generals promised that any former Byzantine lands would be returned to the emperor's control. They would merely be new lords within the Byzantine Empire. Alexios probably didn't trust them to keep their word, but the oath of fealty would be a useful lever to use against them. He conducted them into Turkish territory and waited to see what would happen.

If Alexios was hoping for a repeat of Peter the Hermit's fiasco, he was soon to be disappointed. The Crusaders marched across Asia Minor, first taking Nicaea, then Antioch from the Turks. Once they fought their way through Asia Minor, they turned their attention to the Arabs. By 1099 they made it to Jerusalem, where their religious fanaticism came to full bloom. The Muslim civilians were put to the sword or led away as slaves. The Jews, who had been living peacefully under Muslim dominion, were rounded up, packed into a synagogue, and burned alive.

After this, Alexios was probably not surprised when the Crusaders kept the land for themselves and refused to take orders from Constantinople. Soon Alexios was fighting the very people who had supposedly been sent to save him. But this didn't turn into the great disaster he feared. He was much more successful fighting his fellow Christians than he was against the Turks. The Crusaders were terribly unpopular and needed to keep many of their troops in their newly conquered territories to avert a rebellion. Brutal and intolerant, they were a sharp contrast to the more refined Arabs and Byzantines, both of whom always allowed a bit of social and religious diversity among their population.

To survive this turmoil, Alexios put the empire on a lean regime of massive military spending bolstered by high taxes. Rich and poor were taxed alike, and press gangs prowled the cities and villages for potential "recruits" they could carry off into military service.

Higher taxes always carried the risk of unrest by the urban poor. At this time the danger was even greater because Alexios didn't spend large amounts of money on lavish churches and palaces like some of his predecessors. While expensive, these projects were a good way to employ people. Alexios took the more practical option of building an entire neighborhood of public facilities in Constantinople. There was a giant hospital, a soup kitchen, an orphanage, and a home for the disabled. Government aid to the poor was always a cornerstone of Byzantine policy, but assistance had never been provided in so organized and complete a fashion.

Despite the streamlining of the economy, Alexios still needed outside help. In 1082, he granted Venetian merchants sweeping privileges. They were allowed full freedom of movement and residence within the empire, something not even granted to Byzantine citizens. The central government made it difficult for citizens to move about; it preferred them to be settled, which made them easier to tax. There were tolls on the roads, and a traveler had to prove a valid reason for entering the capital. Merchants were also restricted by various tariffs and local protections.

Foreigners were also given their own neighborhood in Constantinople. Soon wealthy Venetian merchant families built luxurious palaces financed by lucrative trade deals. While this grant encouraged international commerce and gained Byzantium a valuable ally, it also undermined the domestic economy. Byzantine merchants found it difficult to compete and were increasingly marginalized. Alexios died a natural death in 1118 after a rule of nearly forty years. Considering the chaos that preceded him, the long period of stability and the bloodless transfer of power to his son John II Komnenos (1118–43) were perhaps his greatest achievements.

John II was a pious and popular man, and was dubbed "John the Beautiful" by his people. The empire had partially recovered from the disaster of Manzikert, but there were still problems. The Venetians were getting more and more control over Byzantine commerce. They took advantage of their duty-free trading privileges in Constantinople to dominate the Byzantine economy. The Greek merchant class no longer controlled international trade. While the Greeks still ran local commerce, the big profits were made from international trade. Much of that money was now going straight to Venice. In exchange, the Byzantines could call on the powerful Venetian navy in times of danger. The Venetians were an important ally, but domestic pressure gave John no choice but to cancel their favored status. In response, Venetian ships ravaged the coastline. The Venetians, it appeared, were worse enemies than friends. John returned their privileges.

He fared better against the Crusaders and the Turks. From 1130 to 1135, he led annual campaigns against the Turks, making small advances each time. Then he marched on Antioch, once the second city of the empire and now in the hands of French and German knights who were too busy fighting among themselves to organize an adequate defense. The city was surrounded and the leadership of the Kingdom of Jerusalem, the main Crusader authority, decided to give Antioch back to John in the hopes that they could buy his friendship. The Crusader kingdom had been gradually losing land to the Turks and Arabs almost since its foundation and desperately needed allies.

Their submission worked. The Crusaders and the Byzantines fought together against the Muslims, making some gains in Syria before losing them again due to lack of cooperation between the armies.

By the time John's son Manuel (1143–80) came to the throne the Crusaders were doing poorly. They were losing battles to the Byzantines and the Muslims, and could not iron out their internal politics enough to reverse these setbacks. The Crusader kingdoms were poor, unstable, and gradually losing ground. They called for help from the west.

The response was quick in coming. On Christmas Day 1145, King Louis VII of France announced he would lead a Second Crusade. Soon the armies of Europe were marching towards Byzantium once again.

Manuel took a lesson from his grandfather Alexios. He provided food and an armed escort, and insisted on an oath of fealty. The first army to arrive was a German force that plundered its way across eastern Europe. Manuel got them out of Byzantine territory as quickly as he could, and was relieved when the Turks cut them to pieces just past the border.

The French army started a more disciplined march across eastern Europe, but they had the misfortune of coming after the Germans. The local peasantry was in no mood for more Crusaders. The French had to fight their way to Byzantium. When they arrived Manuel promptly shipped them over to Asia Minor. Muslim armies dogged them all the way to Antioch. They arrived decimated and exhausted, their crusading spirit gone. Soon they were taking any available ship back to the west.

Despite their rowdy behavior and battlefield ineptitude, the Crusaders somehow impressed Manuel. He was fascinated by the culture of the "Franks" or "Latins," as the Byzantines called anyone from western Europe. Manuel enjoyed the more relaxed attitude western leaders shared with their subordinates, and soon shocked his own subjects by working alongside his soldiers, even helping out with a shovel when they were digging fortifications. He also held tournaments in the Hippodrome and took his turn jousting with the Latin knights.

There had always been a small community of Latins in Constantinople, mostly merchants trying to compete with the Venetians. Under Manuel the Latin neighborhood expanded dramatically. Latins soon occupied important positions at the imperial court. Because they hailed from different countries, Manuel saw them as less of a threat than the highly organized Venetians, whose merchant quarter was now the wealthiest neighborhood in the capital.

The people saw things differently. To the average Byzantine, westerners were boorish, uneducated (meaning they didn't speak Greek) and, worst of all, Catholic. It is difficult for a modern person to understand how deeply religion was embedded in the medieval mind. To Orthodox Christians, Catholics were worse than Muslims or Jews. Muslims were the infidel, but at least they didn't pretend to be Christians. Jews were second-class citizens, but they were tolerated to a far higher degree in Byzantium than they were in western Europe. Catholics, on the other hand, were wayward Christians constantly trying to undermine the Orthodox Church. Their behavior during the Crusades proved to the Byzantines once and for all that they were thoroughly uncivilized.

The westerners didn't think very highly of the Byzantines either. In their minds, the Orthodox refused to unite the Church, insisting on their strange and Oriental traditions. They even went so far as to deny the supremacy of the pope. To the westerner, Constantinople was like a new Sodom, a wayward city, full of corruption and extravagant wealth. The churches were filled with luminous, lifelike mosaics and paintings that, seen through the haze of incense and flickering candlelight, seemed to float off the wall. The priests officiated over strange and complex rituals, intoning in an incomprehensible language. They looked upon the city with a mixture of awe and repulsion. To a French or a German knight, brought up with tales of the fabulous wealth and glory of Constantinople, to see it in real life must have been a profound shock: to see Jews and Muslims walking the streets, to see Orthodox rites in the churches, to see so much wealth in the hands of a people who denied the authority of the Church in Rome.

This rift between the two Christian peoples would never be bridged. Few tried. There were occasional marriages and even conversions, but those were rare. Eastern and western scholars would not discover each other until the last days of the empire, when the

Dome mosaic showing Christ Pantocrator, Panagia tou Arakos, Lagoudera, Cyprus, late twelfth century. Pantokrator is Greek for "Ruler of All," a term applied to God in Revelation 19:6. Christ Pantokrator was shown holding the Gospels in his left hand while blessing with his right.

SOURCE: Dumbarton Oaks, Byzantine Photograph and Fieldwork Archives, Washington, DC. Photograph by Richard Anderson.

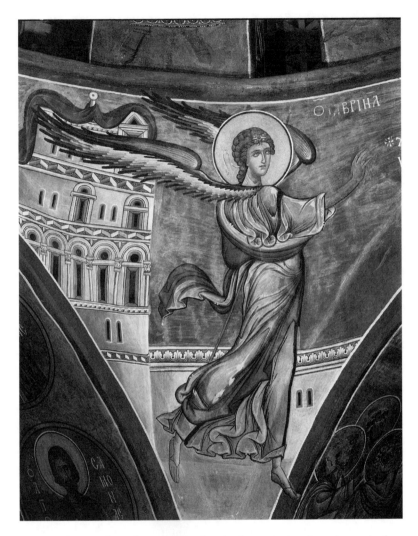

Painting showing the archangel Gabriel at the Annunciation, Panagia tou Arakos, Lagoudera, Cyprus, 1192. Some churches were decorated with paintings as well as mosaics. This one shows an unusually expressive style.

SOURCE: Dumbarton Oaks, Byzantine Photograph and Fieldwork Archives, Washington, DC. Photograph by Richard Anderson.

first years of the Renaissance saw a renewed interest in the classical culture to which the Byzantines were heir. The priests never moved beyond vituperative debate. The vast space between the two worlds would remain. The western peoples would allow the eastern peoples to eventually be absorbed by the Turks, and the distinction between an Eastern and Western Europe is still part of our concept of the world today.

Manuel, the most pro-western emperor Byzantium ever had, died in 1180. Mistrust and animosity between east and west, between Catholic and Orthodox, was as strong as ever. Twenty-five years later that schism would nearly destroy the empire.

The new emperor was Manuel's son Alexios II (1180–83). He was only eleven, so the government was run by his mother, Manuel's widow, Marie of Antioch. Manuel's interest in the west had extended to women as well—Marie was one of the dreaded Latins. She was the daughter of the French crusader Raymond, prince of Antioch. The city had once been one of the most important in the Byzantine empire, but it was once again in the hands of the crusaders. To the Byzantines her presence was bad enough, but when she increased Latin trading concessions and posted westerners to influential positions at the court, their rage could not be contained.

The mob found a focus in the person of Andronikos Komnenos, a cousin of the boy emperor. He came to the capital and declared that he would protect Alexios from the Latins. Rioters poured into the streets, breaking into the Latin Quarter, looting the houses and killing the occupants. Andronikos rode a wave of popular support and soon isolated and dominated Alexios, forcing him to order Marie's execution and to declare Andronikos co-emperor. Once the empress-regent was out of the way, Alexios didn't have long to live. Late in 1183, Andronikos' servants strangled the boy.

Andronikos (1183–85) was frustrated by the endemic corruption in the Byzantine bureaucracy. He warned his officials that they didn't have long to live if they continued their corruption. He managed to expunge the worst of it, but made many political enemies in the process. Officials had become rich off of bribes and kickbacks, and didn't appreciate having to follow the rules.

His popularity with the common people didn't last. An army of Normans from Sicily appeared outside Thessaloniki, one of Byzantium's richest cities, and took it by storm. The Normans were not satisfied with merely abusing the citizenry, but turned their wrath on the Orthodox churches, urinating on altars and using holy icons as kindling for their cooking fires. Andronikos' reputation as the protector of the Orthodox Church from the Latins was ruined.

Soon the city mob in Constantinople raised up Isaac II Angelos (1185–95) as their choice for emperor. Andronikos sent an official to arrest the pretender to the throne, but Isaac drew his sword and cut the official down. Then he ran through the city streets, bloody sword in hand, shouting "Follow me!" Andronikos was caught and given over to the tender mercies of the mob. Unfortunately for him, the mob's tortures lasted most of the day.

Isaac immediately sent a force to repulse the Normans. While the Byzantines fought a Norman army sent out to face them, the people of Thessaloniki rose up and slaughtered the Norman garrison.

Isaac was remarkably different from Andronikos. He lived a luxurious lifestyle, often wearing a robe only once before throwing it away. He was even rumored to bathe every other day, an unheard-of indulgence. All the robes and baths apparently added up, and he began to sell government offices to keep up with his household expenses. He even levied a special tax to finance his wedding to the princess of Hungary.

Isaac founded the Angeli dynasty, a short-lived and ineffective dynasty that would end in disaster. Its rulers tended to be weak, and the empire was plagued with regional rebellions.

His foreign policy was little better. Jerusalem fell to the Muslims in 1187. The Saracen general Saladin took the city with little effort, showing just how far the Crusader kingdom had degenerated through infighting and mismanagement. Unlike the Crusaders, Saladin showed mercy on the city's inhabitants. The city was not plundered, and most of the citizens were able to buy their freedom. Despite this chivalric gesture, the pope died of shock when he heard the news. The new pope immediately called for a Third Crusade.

This wall painting shows St. Neophytos being raised to Heaven by the archangels Michael and Gabriel. Neophytos was an ascetic who carved a home and chapel on a cliff in Cyprus. Artists painted this scene in 1182 or 1183 shortly after his death. It became a holy spot and the monastery of St. Neophytos was founded there.

SOURCE: Dumbarton Oaks, Byzantine Photograph and Fieldwork Archives, Washington, DC.

Isaac was worried. Knowing the effect of the previous two Crusades, and hearing reports that the new armies assembling were the largest yet, he urgently tried to dissuade them from coming by way of Constantinople. Fortunately for Byzantium, most of the Crusaders chose a sea route, but one army had to be shipped at Byzantine expense. The Third Crusade achieved little more than the Second. The army that marched along the land route was predictably defeated. Those that arrived in the Holy Land by sea were unable to retake Jerusalem.

Isaac had problems closer to home as well. The Bulgars rose up in a series of rebellions in the 1180s and eventually broke away, establishing the second Bulgarian empire. Isaac campaigned for several years to recapture the lost territory, but Bulgaria had evolved into a powerful, centralized kingdom. It would never again be a Byzantine province.

By 1195, the once-popular emperor had lost his credibility. The people of Byzantium never tolerated failures on the throne. Isaac was deposed and blinded by his brother Alexios III (1195–1203), but he turned out to be no better as a ruler. Eager to please Venice, he allowed legal disputes between Byzantines and Venetians to be tried by Venetian judges, a remarkable concession to a foreign power. Alexios proved equally weak against the Germans. When the emperor of Germany threatened to invade, Alexios panicked and plundered the imperial tombs in order to buy him off. The Germans decided to invade anyway, but their plans were stopped when their ruler died suddenly. Alexios lost nothing but his dignity.

Once again the Byzantine people showed their impatience with bad rulers. When Alexios III had blinded his brother, he had intended to do the same to his nephew Alexios IV. The boy managed to escape by dressing as a Latin and slipping away on an Italian ship. He spent several years in the west, gaining allies. By 1203, he was back, supported by a Venetian fleet carrying an army of Crusaders.

This Crusade, the Fourth, started badly. The Crusaders hired the Venetians to have ships waiting for them when they arrived in Italy, but they failed to gather enough recruits to pay. The doge of Venice, already in his eighties and completely blind, made them an offer. He and some of his soldiers would join the Crusade for a share of the spoils. The Crusaders then could pay their debt with what they got from the Holy Land. Their first stop, however, would be the Balkan city of Zara, a former Venetian territory that had rebelled and joined with the Hungarians. The doge wanted it back, and the Crusaders would have to help him. The first battle of the Fourth Crusade would be against Christians. Soon the army set sail. They retook Zara, killing most of the Hungarian garrison, then turned their wrath on the city's inhabitants. When the pope heard of the atrocities they committed against fellow Catholics, he excommunicated the entire army.

At this point Alexios IV appeared. He offered to help fund the expedition if they would help him take the throne from his uncle. He also offered to put the Orthodox Church under papal authority. For the Crusaders this proposal was a wonderful offer. Not only would it solve their monetary problems, which apparently had not been alleviated by the sack of Zara, but it would surely get the pope to forgive them.

The fleet arrived at Constantinople in the summer of 1203 to find the city completely unprepared. The Golden Horn, the city's port, was blocked by a great chain that could be raised and lowered to allow ships to pass. But the mechanism for the chain was guarded by a single, undermanned tower. The tower was soon taken, the chain lowered, and the Venetian fleet sailed in, destroying the Byzantine navy before it had time to get ready. While the city's land walls were all but impregnable, the walls facing the harbor were shorter and thinner.

Now the city was completely encircled. The Crusaders were desperate for a quick victory. It was July, but besieging a city could take months and the invaders did not want to be caught outside the walls in the winter like so many of their predecessors. The Greeks charged out of the gates half a dozen times a day to raid the Crusader camp. The Crusaders had to sleep in their armor. These constant attacks kept the soldiers from foraging for food. Geoffroy de Villehardouin, a French knight who wrote a chronicle of the Fourth Crusade, describes the situation.

> " . . . we were extremely short of supplies, except for flour and bacon, and very little indeed of these. The troops had no fresh meat at all, except what they got from the horses that were killed. There was, in fact, only sufficient food for the next three weeks. Our army was thus in an extremely desperate situation, for never, in any city, have so many been besieged by so few." [1]

The Crusaders were getting desperate. An all-out attack was their only hope. While the French and Germans assaulted the land walls, the Venetians brought their ships up to the sea walls. Catapults on the ships kept up a constant hail of stones and made it hazardous for any defender to show himself. Then the Venetians brought up scaling ladders. The Greeks fought back hard for an entire day, hurling stones and arrows down on the attackers and pushing the ladders, men and all, into the sea.

The Venetians pressed on, and eventually got control of much of the sea wall. The Greeks fled and the Venetians charged into the city. Emperor Alexios rallied his men and a bloody street fight ensued. The Venetians fell back. Afraid they'd be pushed out of the city altogether, the Venetians set fire to the houses between them and the Greeks, creating an impassible wall of fire. A wind was blowing off the bay and carried the flames deeper into the city.

At this point Alexios III lost his nerve. That night he slipped away with his retinue and as much of the imperial treasury as they could carry. When the people of Constantinople discovered their emperor had betrayed them, they went to the prison and released the deposed emperor Isaac II. Although he had been blinded by Alexios II eight years before, the palace officials and the people declared him their ruler.

---

1. Villehardouin, "Conquest of Constantinople," pp. 68–69. Reproduced by permission of Penguin Books, Ltd.

Isaac began negotiations with the Crusaders. He said that since he was, after all, the rightful ruler, his son Alexios IV didn't have a claim. Isaac was blind, which was usually not acceptable in a Byzantine ruler, but the doge could hardly object to that. A compromise was reached in which he would reign as co-emperor with his son Alexios IV (1203–4). The Byzantines would also pay off the Crusaders' debt to the Venetians and supply them with ships and men to help with the Crusade.

The co-emperors tried desperately to pay, but the treasury was nearly empty and the capital ravaged. They taxed the people as much as they could, and even confiscated valuable ceremonial objects from the churches, but the money collected was nowhere near enough. In the meantime, the Latins wandered the streets, bullying the citizens and showing disrespect to the Orthodox churches and clergy. A group of Crusaders were shocked to find a Muslim neighborhood with its own mosque. They set the mosque on fire, starting a huge conflagration that reduced a large portion of the city to ashes.

After this, a coup was inevitable. Isaac and Alexios IV were murdered and a new emperor, Alexios V Doukas (1204) took power. He defied the Crusaders, forbidding them entry to the city and telling them that they could expect no more money.

Now the Crusaders and the doge decided they wanted more than money, they wanted Constantinople itself. Again they launched an assault on the sea walls, for they still controlled the harbor, and again they were successful.

What happened next was the worst disaster in the city's history.

"Then followed a scene of massacre and pillage: on every hand the Greeks were cut down, their horses, palfreys, mules, and other possessions snatched as booty. So great was the number killed that no man could count them . . . fire began to take hold of the city, which was soon blazing fiercely, and went on burning the whole of the night and all the next day till evening. This was the third fire there had been in Constantinople since the French and Venetians arrived in the land, and more houses had been burnt in that city than there are in any three of the greatest cities in the kingdom of France."[2]

Alexios V managed to escape. Alexios III called him to his hiding place to offer him a truce, then betrayed and blinded him. The Crusaders captured Alexios V shortly thereafter, and executed him by pushing him from the column of Theodosius in Constantinople.

The capital had fallen, but not the empire. Much of its territory was still in Greek hands, and there were several claimants to the throne hiding out in the countryside. The people would not renounce Orthodoxy to their hated Catholic rulers. A Greek emperor would once again rule the New Rome. But before that would happen Byzantium would suffer the worst half century of its long history.

---

2. Villehardouin, "Conquest of Constantinople," pp. 91–92. Reproduced by permission of Penguin Books, Ltd.

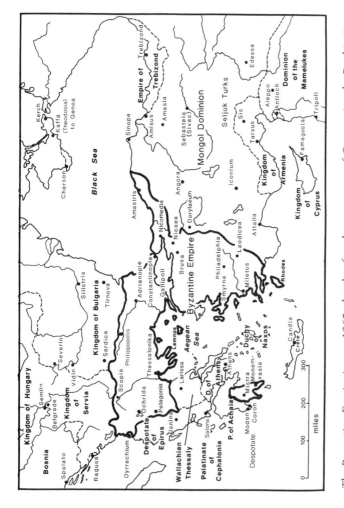

The Byzantine Empire in A.D. 1265, shortly after the reconquest of Constantinople. By this time the empire had shrunk to a fraction of its former size.

SOURCE: *Byzantium: Church, Society and Civilization Seen through Contemporary Eyes*, by Deno John Geanakoplos (University of Chicago Press, 1984).

VII.

OCCUPATION AND DECLINE

(1204–1448)

———◆———

For the two generations of Constantinopolitans who lived under Latin rule, it must have seemed like their world had come to an end. Great swaths of the city were charred ruins. The Latins only rebuilt what they reserved for their own use. Many of the churches that survived the flames were desecrated and then turned over to Catholic clergy. The Catholic priesthood harangued and persecuted the Byzantines, trying to get them to renounce their faith. The secular rulers, living in palaces with large retinues of Greek slaves, wrung extortionate taxes from the people.

But the Byzantines held on. The lucky ones were able to flee to one of the three independent states that were all that remained of their old empire. Each was ruled by a claimant to the Byzantine throne. The largest and closest was centered around the wealthy city of Nicaea, and controlled much of the rich lands of northwestern Asia Minor. Another state was based in northern Greece around Epiros, while the third was the distant outpost of Trebizond, on the southern shore of the Black Sea.

Those left in the city had little hope. Occasionally news trickled in of fights between the free Byzantines and the Crusaders, but these skirmishes usually ended in Latin victories. The Byzantine elite, true to form, were even now fighting among themselves and could not make a united front against the invaders. Still, most Byzantines

131

resisted the Catholic Church's repeated attempts to convert them. If their lives under occupation were miserable, at least they could rest assured that their souls were safe. Those who gave in found themselves shunned by their countrymen and mistrusted by the Latins.

The new rulers of Constantinople were remarkably incapable of handling their own affairs. They were chronically short of money, and even resorted to selling Christ's crown of thorns, one of the most treasured relics of the empire, to the Venetians. When the money from that sale ran out, the Crusaders resorted to hawking the lead roof of the imperial palace to a scrap merchant.

The empire of Nicaea was biding its time. Under the capable Laskarid dynasty, it reorganized itself into a miniature version of Byzantium, with its own patriarch, an army based on the theme system, and an imperial court. Its emperors made no hasty moves, preferring to act defensively and grabbing what little gains they could when their enemies were weak. Their biggest windfall was recapturing Thessaloniki, in southern Greece, in 1246. The city was the main port for the Balkans and was the richest city in the region besides Constantinople.

The Laskarid rulers were famously thrifty. One of them raised chickens and bought his wife a crown from the proceeds. The people called it her "egg crown." The Laskarids also sent scouts to Constantinople to keep up to date on the situation.

In 1261, one of these scouting parties learned that the Crusader army had left Constantinople and sailed off with the Venetian navy to capture a nearby island. The city was lightly guarded. Even more promising, the Latins neglected to lock a small, little-used gate in the city walls.

The scouts sent word back to a larger Greek force camped nearby. Together they slipped into the city. They overpowered the few Latin guards and opened one of the main gates to allow a backup force to gallop through. The city was theirs. The Byzantines burnt the Venetian quarter to the ground and herded every Venetian and Latin they could find down to the harbor.

When the Venetian navy returned, they found their homes destroyed and their families waiting for them on the piers. There was

Reliquary cross with Crucifixion, gold and cloisonné enamel, Thessaloniki, late twelfth-early thirteenth century. The cloisonné technique was a Byzantine speciality and involved fixing enamel or precious stones into raised metal settings. Reliquary crosses such as this one were hollow and would contain a holy object such as a saint's bone or a fragment of the True Cross.

nothing they could do but gather their loved ones and leave. Remembering how they had treated the Greeks a half century before, they must have considered themselves fortunate.

The first Byzantine emperor to sit on the throne in liberated Constantinople again was Michael VIII Palaiologos (1261–82). He was the founder of a new dynasty, the Palaiologoi, which would be the longest-lasting dynasty in Byzantine history. Sadly, the rule of the Palaiologoi encompassed some of the darkest years. Michael had an unseemly past. As a general in Nicaea, he staged a coup by blinding the previous emperor, a young boy of the Laskarid family whom he had pledged to protect. He was excommunicated by the patriarch for this act, but Michael simply removed the man from office and found a more cooperative member of the clergy. His self-serving deeds were not good for his popularity. His appeal dipped even lower when he suggested a union with Rome.

To the Byzantines the suggestion of such an alliance was an outrage. They had suffered too much at the hands of the Catholics. But, taking a longer perspective, it is easy to see why Michael acted as he did. The pope could call a new Crusade at any time, and the small and weak Byzantine army would stand little chance of resisting it. Michael strung along three successive popes with vague promises of union for more than a decade. He saved the empire from another attack, but his people saw him as a traitor to the faith.

He also tried to find allies in the Italians. He made a close alliance with Genoa, a rising city-state hungry for a share of the eastern trade. He even allowed the Venetians back into Constantinople. The two communities now competed with each other, and soon built large and prosperous trading colonies in and around the capital. The tax revenue these colonies generated helped revive a little of the empire's old wealth.

By 1274, Michael could delay the Vatican no longer. The French king was threatening to lead another Crusade against Byzantium. Michael and the Catholic Church had a council in Lyons, France, to discuss the matter of union. The Byzantines were allowed to keep the parts of their liturgy that didn't conflict with Catholic doctrine, and the service would continue to be in Greek instead of Latin, but in

Hagia Sophia, Trebizond (modern Trabzon): Built on the site of a Roman temple of Apollo, the present structure probably was built by Grand Komnenos Manuel I (1238–43), a member of the prominent Komnenos family, not to be confused with his imperial ancestor of the same name from the previous century. The Komnenoi fled to Trebizond, on the southern shore of the Black Sea, after the Crusaders took Constantinople. During their rule they founded many churches and monuments in the region. Tradition holds that the later Manuel is buried here. The church originally served a long-gone monastery.

SOURCE: Turkish Tourist Office.

Monastery of Constantine Lips (Fenari Isa Camii), exterior view of the east end of the south church, Constantinople, 1280s. As brickwork became popular, artisans created complex designs on the exteriors of buildings.

SOURCE: Dumbarton Oaks, Byzantine Photograph and Fieldwork Archives, Washington, DC. Photograph by Thomas F. Matthews.

important matters—Papal authority and the nature of the Trinity— they had to submit to Rome. Michael agreed, and at the Council of Lyons the two churches were united. The reaction in Constantinople was immediate and heartfelt. The western Church they hated was once again in control of their immortal souls. The fact that Michael saved the empire from almost certain destruction didn't matter to them. Their faith was more important. "Better the sultan's turban than the cardinal's mitre" became a popular expression.[1] Michael, somehow, kept his throne. Perhaps the Byzantines had seen too much upheaval in the past few generations to stage a coup. Nevertheless, virtually no one converted. Michael launched a bitter campaign of religious persecution to force the union of Churches, but it did no good. Many religious leaders preferred imprisonment and mutilation to conversion.

When Michael died in 1282, his son Andronikos II (1282–1328) buried him in a secret location outside the city. The man who had restored the capital was buried in shame and exile, a heretic in the eyes of his people.

Andronikos' first act after rising to the throne was to repeal the Union of Lyons. He emptied the prisons of religious dissidents, and the people were once again free to worship according to the Orthodox rite. Andronikos II did not want to be as unpopular as his father. The only way to win the hearts of the people was to be an Orthodox emperor. The western Catholic Church was concerned with its own internal strife at the time, and for a few decades the Byzantines were free from Rome.

But Andronikos II could not ignore the powerful landlords and monasteries in the countryside. During the occupation of Constantinople, when there was no strong, central authority, they gained a great deal of power. The monasteries were almost autonomous states, with no law but Orthodox law, and the rural lords spent most of their energies fighting amongst themselves rather than dealing with external enemies. Andronikos was never able to assert the kind of authority that emperors did before the Crusades. His successors fared

---

1. Norwich, *A Short History of Byzantium*, p. 317.

Fresco of Christ in the Chora Monastery, fourteenth century. This monastery, built just outside the walls of Constantinople, was founded in the sixth century but extensively restored in the fourteenth century by Theodore Metochites, a scholar and advisor to Emperor Andronikos II. When Andronikos II was deposed, Metochites retired to the monastery and spent his entire fortune redecorating it.

SOURCE: Laura Hollengreen.

Mosaic, Theodore Metochites before Christ, Kariye Camii, Constantinople, 1321. Even in the Palaeologian period Byzantine artisans created fabulous mosaics. Here the donor of the church offers a model of the building to Christ. Metochites is shown in the traditional noble dress of the period.

SOURCE: Dumbarton Oaks, Byzantine Photograph and Fieldwork Archives, Washington, DC.

little better. The last few rulers of Byzantium would not be auto-crats like their ancestors; they would rule a dwindling and deeply divided state.

While repealing the union brought him popularity, Andronikos' next act made far less sense. Finding the imperial treasury nearly empty, he ordered deep cuts in the military budget and abolished the navy altogether. To do this at the very time that the Turks were reor-ganizing and the western powers were contemplating reprisals for the break with Rome, was considered little short of mad. Many of the Byzantine sailors and shipbuilders found work with the Turks, and soon built them their first navy.

Andronikos assumed the Genoese would defend Byzantium's shores. After all, they had a wealthy trading colony at Galata, just across the Golden Horn from Constantinople. Most merchant ships docked there and paid their dues directly into Italian coffers. But the Italians always had their own priorities. They defended Byzantine interests only when it helped their profits.

Andronikos was soon to regret his mistake. A new tribe of Turks was becoming dominant in Asia Minor. They called themselves Ottomans after their leader Othman. His dynasty would make that name the fear of the Christian world. They defeated Greeks and Turks alike and gained a foothold in Thrace, on the European side of the Bosphorus. Refugees crowded into the capital, sleeping in the streets and the once-great public buildings abandoned from an ear-lier age. The emperor had no army capable of facing the threat. Instead, he hired a Spanish mercenary band called the Grand Com-pany of Catalans.

At first all went well. The mercenaries turned out to be fierce fighters and pushed back the Ottomans. But they liked pillaging Greek towns as much as the Turks did. The Byzantines faced the same problem as before, but now they were paying for the privilege. The Catalans even let Turkish warriors help them. Together they looted the monasteries and churches on Mt. Athos, a massive monastery complex in Greece that was one of the spiritual centers of the Orthodox Church. They also besieged Thessaloniki, but failed to take it. Byzantium was only saved when the Catalans marched off to Greece and set up a duchy in Athens in 1311.

Andronikos ruled nearly fifty years. By the time his grandson Andronikos III (1328–41) deposed him, most of the lands in Asia Minor were in the hands of the Ottomans. The empire now controlled only part of Thrace, whose towns were mostly rubble, and the Morea region in the Peloponnese. The Ottomans were steadily advancing across Asia Minor. The last thin strip of Byzantium's wealthy Asian provinces was rapidly disappearing. Nicaea, one of the most important cities still in the empire and the site of its religious foundation, fell in 1331. Two years later, Andronikos III agreed to pay the Ottomans an annual tribute. As Byzantine emperors had done so many times before, he bought off the enemies he couldn't defeat.

The emperor tried to regain some initiative. He retook much of northern Greece, which was holding out as an independent kingdom, but the victory was short-lived. Serbia took the land in 1330. This Christian kingdom started out as a Byzantine province before breaking away in 1168. It had been steadily expanding its influence in the Balkans. Now that the Bulgars were weak, there was no one else to compete with the Serbs. The Byzantine emperor also restored the navy, although he could not afford to make it large enough to do much more than patrol the coast and islands near the capital. He managed to get his family into influential positions in the Church and rural aristocracy. While he could not attain the supremacy of earlier emperors, at least much of the power was kept within the family.

Andronikos III died in 1341. His son John V was still underage, so he was dominated by the powerful minister John Cantacuzene. A bitter civil war broke out between Cantacuzene and Anna, Andronikos' widow, who objected to the minister's power. Cantacuzene won after several bloody years of fighting and the two Johns were crowned co-emperors in 1347. John V Palaiologos didn't like the minister's domination either, and after much political maneuvering he forced John Canatcuzene to step down in 1354.

Nor was all this infighting the only problem facing the empire. In 1346 a terrible earthquake rocked the capital. The dome of the Hagia

Ivory pyxis, with ceremonial scenes of the family of John Cantacuzene, Constantinople, early fifteenth century. A pyxis is a box made with a section of elephant tusk. Ivory was a favored material for Byzantine artists and came from two sources: the elephants of Africa and the narwhals of Scandinavia.
SOURCE: Dumbarton Oaks, Byzantine Photograph and Fieldwork Archives, Washington, DC.

Sophia was damaged, but there was no money to repair it. The next year the Black Death, a terrible epidemic of bubonic plague, swept into Constantinople from Asia. It spread through fleas on rats, common in the unsanitary conditions of medieval cities. It killed half of Constantinople's population. Ships passing through the city's extensive trading network became infested with rats from shore, and when the ships returned home their furry stowaways unwittingly spread the disease to the rest of Europe. A third of Europe died.

Byzantium was now on its knees. The countryside was ravaged and bankrupt. Constantinople never fully recovered from the Latin occupation. Many neighborhoods were never rebuilt and large areas inside the walls became pasture or orchards. Even the crown jewels were gone, pawned to the Venetians in a vain attempt to win their support against the Turks. Now the "True Emperor of the Romans" wore a crown of glass.

Commerce suffered too. The Turks blocked the main land route to Asia; caravans had difficulty getting through. What little trade went on in the capital was dominated by the Venetians and the Genoese. Galata, the Genoese trading colony, was estimated to have seven times the wealth of Constantinople. Thessaloniki still prospered since it was the main port for the Balkans, but many of its public structures were destroyed during an uprising of people calling themselves the Zealots.

The Zealots were tired of the constant infighting among the nobility, which always hurt the common people the most. From 1342–50 the Zealots took over Thessaloniki and much of Thrace, plundering the houses of the rich and setting up their own government. The Zealot rebellion was similar to the many of the peasant uprisings occurring during this time across western Europe, but it was unique in Byzantine history because of its purpose and location. Rebellions had been mostly limited to the capital. Their goal had always been to usurp an unpopular ruler, not change the social order. The faith of the people in their government was obviously shaken.

Some people even lost faith in the Orthodox Church. Greeks in the borderlands converted to Islam. They realized the best way to advance in Muslim society was to be a Muslim. With few opportunities left in Byzantium, some people took on the religion of the empire's enemies.

The time had come for decisive action. In 1366, John V sailed out of Constantinople to seek help from the western provinces. For the first time, a Byzantine emperor ventured beyond the borders without an army. His first stop was the Catholic kingdom of Hungary, where the king told him what he should have already known—no help could be expected without a union of Churches. On his way back through Bulgaria the Bulgars forbade him to leave. They were at peace with the Byzantines at the time, but they hoped to pressure the emperor to give them some political advantage. He was released only when a fleet headed by his cousin attacked the Bulgarian Black Sea coast.

John returned to Constantinople, his last illusions shattered. There was no choice but to submit to the Catholic Church. He knew the Byzantines would never accept it, but he hoped his own conversion might be enough. So in 1370 he left again, this time for Rome. In an elegant ceremony in front of St. Peter's Basilica in Rome, he bowed to the pope and became a Catholic. On his way back home he stopped in Venice, only to realize he didn't have enough money to make it back to Constantinople because he needed to pay his debts to the Venetians. He couldn't do that either, so he ended up in prison. Once again he had to be helped out by a friendly relative.

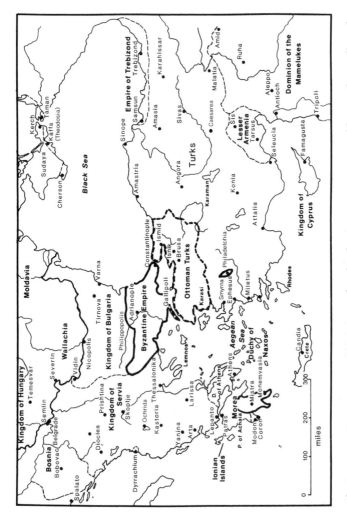

The Byzantine Empire in A.D. *1355. Soon after this the Ottoman empire would expand into all neighboring territories, including Byzantium.*

SOURCE: *Byzantium: Church, Society and Civilization Seen through Contemporary Eyes,* by Deno John Geanakoplos (University of Chicago Press, 1984).

When John V finally returned to Constantinople he met a cold reception. In the next four years he was deposed twice. For three years he was a prisoner while his own son ruled in his stead. He gained his position back but was briefly deposed by his grandson. Although he was always able to regain his throne, the people hated him. The Byzantines saw John V's Catholicism as a betrayal. As emperor, he was head of the Orthodox Church, the leader of God's one true instrument on Earth. Now he had abandoned his post.

No help came from the western states. The rulers there saw little reason to save the new "Catholic" Byzantium from the Muslims. They knew that one of the only Catholics in Byzantium was its ruler, and he was the most unpopular man in the empire.

The Turks were now spreading into the Balkans, pushing back the Bulgars and Serbs. John took the only option left to him—he became the sultan's vassal. His lands were nearly surrounded by the Ottomans, and he saw submission as the only alternative to inevitable defeat. As a precaution he improved the city walls, but he was again foiled. One of John's sons was staying at the Ottoman court as a "guest," basically a pampered hostage, a common type of diplomatic insurance during the Middle Ages. The sultan warned that if the new defenses weren't destroyed, he would pluck the young man's eyes out. John had no choice but to obey his new master. The emperor became a recluse, his will sapped from him. He shut himself in the palace and died a few months later.

The Ottomans advanced quickly in Europe. The Bulgarian trading center Sofia fell in 1382, and the capital Turnovo in 1393. Then Mt. Athos, the monastic center of Orthodoxy, became part of the Ottoman Empire. In 1387 the Turks took the Byzantine port of Thessaloniki. The Serbian empire, the most powerful Christian force in the region, suffered a serious defeat in 1389 at the Field of the Blackbirds. In 1390 the Turks captured Philadelphia, the last Greek city in Asia. Byzantium's turn was coming in only a matter of time.

The next emperor, Manuel II (1391–1425), tried to stand up to the Turks. When called by the sultan to help him invade Europe, he refused. Instead he called on the western powers to start a new crusade against the Muslims. No one listened to him, but they did listen to the more powerful king of Hungary, whose country now bordered the Ottoman Empire and was obviously its next target. In 1396 the members of the campaign gathered a coalition of Germans, French, Hungarians, and Wallachians (Romanians), along with smaller contingents from kingdoms as far away as England. Their army boasted one hundred thousand men. It was never officially called a crusade by the pope, but Manuel called it that in order to gain volunteers. This campaign was the largest one against the expanding Ottoman empire, and the shortest. At their first meeting with the Turks the westerners were butchered. Most of the men were taken prisoner, and the sultan ordered ten thousand of them decapitated while he watched.

The Ottomans then built the great castle of Anadolu Hisar, meaning "the Asian castle," dominating the Asiatic shore of the Bosphorus and within sight of Constantinople. The stronghold was an obvious threat to the city and its commercial lifeline. Manuel sent urgent appeals to the western provinces. The response was lukewarm, so in 1399 he set out personally.

Manuel was very popular in the western kingdoms. Europe was in the first early glimmerings of the Renaissance, and the emperor of the Romans, with his sharp wit and extensive knowledge of Greek classics, became a celebrity. He was entertained in grand style wherever he went. In France he dazzled the scholars at the Sorbonne with his quotes from ancient writers. The king of England set up collection boxes in all the churches in his country to raise money for a new Crusade. Manuel was dined and feted as the defender of Christianity. But in practical terms the western states did very little. Besides some money, all Manuel got was well-phrased excuses.

Manuel returned to his tiny empire. He had gone farther than any other Byzantine ruler in search of help, but he came back as empty-handed as the rest of them. He kept the land in good working order and tried to placate the Ottoman Turks. Fortunately for him, they were occupied with the Tatars, a fierce tribe of horsemen related to the Mongols. The Tatars were led by Tamerlane, a brilliant general who had already conquered much of Persia, fought his way north to the Volga river, and reached as far as India in the east. Tamerlane then attacked the Ottomans, capturing Aleppo and Baghdad and making the Ottoman sultan his prisoner.

Because of their weakened state, Manuel was able to make a treaty with the Turks that got back Mt. Athos and Thessaloniki, and ended the tribute the Byzantines had been paying ever since their first submission as vassals. While the treaty would only last as long as the Tatars remained a threat, it gave Manuel some breathing space.

But the end was in sight. Many Greeks decided to leave Byzantium for safer places in the west. One of Manuel's close friends, Demetrius Kydones, converted to Catholicism and took Venetian citizenship, as he says, "preferring to hear his country's bad news from abroad."[2] Even the emperor's own brother, Theodore Palaiologos, asked Venice for permission to settle there if Constantinople should fall.

Many ordinary people were going west as well. Skilled laborers and artisans found ready work in the booming economies of Renaissance Italy and contributed their talent and knowledge to that vital period of Western civilization. In the first quarter of the fifteenth century the Arsenal, Venice's great shipbuilding center, was run by Greeks. While the tiny Byzantine navy, reinstated after the reign of Andronikos II, could barely defend the capital, these expatriate shipbuilders created the largest fleet Italy had ever seen.

Byzantines went to other cities as well. There was a Greek community in Naples, and after the Council of Ferrara-Florence in 1439 nominally brought the Catholic and Orthodox Churches together, many supporters of union found they were no longer welcome in Byzantium and moved to Rome.

Unlike in the west, classical-style secular education didn't die out during the Middle Ages in Byzantium. Well-educated Byzantines grew up learning the works of ancient Greek philosophers and historians, just the sort of thing that interested Renaissance Italians. Byzantine scholars translated many ancient poets into Latin for the first time. Plato, known to every educated westerner but rarely read

---

2. Harris, "Byzantines in Renaissance Italy," p. 3.

for scarcity of his material, became widely available in Italy thanks to immigrant translators.

Manuel ruled until he was an old man. In his later years, his hair and long beard turned pure white, and he wore white clothes to match. White was the Byzantine color of mourning. No one needed to ask what he was mourning for. He died in 1425.

Despite the grim political picture, Byzantine culture continued to flourish as strongly as before, although on a smaller scale. The Palaiologan Renaissance, as historians call it, started during the Latin occupation of Constantinople. This period saw a great flowering of arts and culture. Impoverished cities and provinces were still willing to support the building of small but beautiful churches and delicately painted icons whose artistic elements resonate in Orthodox art to this day. In philosophy there was a new expansion of ideas, exemplified in its most radical form by George Gemistus Plethon. In the last years of Byzantium, Plethon advocated a neopagan revival strangely reminiscent of Julian. He called for a renewal of the old Greek gods as the only salvation for Byzantine society. His works were burned after his death, but not without respectful speeches on the corruption of a brilliant mind.

The empire seemed spent as a political force, but Byzantines were filled with a new appreciation of their Hellenic roots. Scholars delved deeply into a wide range of subjects; traditional pursuits such as rhetoric and philosophy found new life. Academies were set up to pass their learning along to the next generation, and even a distant outpost like Trebizond had an academy of astronomy by 1300. At these centers of learning, Greek scholars read translations of Persian and Arabic works alongside the classics of Euclid and Homer. Scholars were patronized by the elite and kept in contact with each other through erudite letters written in a Greek imitating the style of Plato and Socrates. The Byzantines rallied to their traditional values as their empire decayed around them.

Caught up in this national pride, Manuel's son John VIII (1425–48) decided that if the empire's remaining days were few, they would at least be glorious. He strengthened the army as much as he could. But he knew that he couldn't succeed alone. He, too, decided

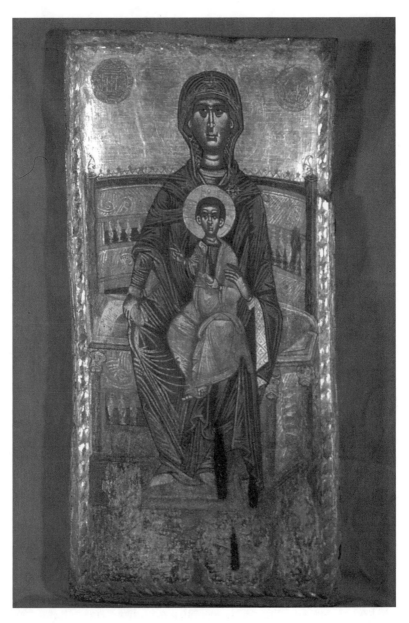

Icon of the Virgin and Child enthroned, fifteenth century. This Greek icon, painted in the last days of the empire, shows Mary in her role as Pantanassa, "Queen of all." The Christ Child's halo is inscribed with the words "the one who is," the divine name revealed to Moses in Exodus 3:14. This icon is gesso (plaster of Paris or gypsum used in painting), paint, and gilt on wood. The gilt is used as a background, similar to the gold backgrounds found on many Byzantine mosaics.

SOURCE: The Malcove Collection, University of Toronto Art Centre, Toronto, Canada.

to travel west, arranging an ecumenical council with the Catholic Church to discuss the possibility of another union. The Byzantines had always insisted on such a council. Only the authority of the entire Church could decide articles of faith. The patriarchs of Constantinople, Alexandria, Antioch, and Jerusalem all attended, as did the pope. With a small army of clergy, scholars, and nobility John went to Italy to see if he could come to an understanding with the pope.

They met in Ferrara in 1438 and, when a plague struck, moved to Florence in 1439. The main issues were the primacy of the pope over the patriarch in Constantinople, and part of the Catholic Creed which states *"Credo in Spiritum Sanctum qui ex patre filioque procedit"* ("I believe in the Holy Spirit who proceeds from the Father and Son"). The point of contention was the term *filioque,* meaning "and Son." The Catholics felt it meant that the Trinity was equal, but the Byzantines objected because they viewed the Trinity as being headed by the Father. They also objected to the fact that this part of the Creed had been adopted by the Catholics without the sanction of an ecumenical council.

After long and heartfelt debates, they reached an agreement. The Orthodox delegates agreed to Papal primacy, and that the Holy Spirit proceeded from the Father "through the Son." The Catholics took this to mean "from the Son," meaning that the Orthodox Church was now in agreement with the Catholic Creed. The Greeks were left to interpret it as they saw fit. The compromise, called the Union of Florence, ended 437 years of division.

The Byzantine people were no more willing to join the Catholic Church than they had been under Michael. Their opinion was exactly the opposite of their emperor's. While he believed union would bring military aid and save the empire, his people felt that to compromise their faith would destroy everything they were trying to defend. If the Orthodox way of life was to die out, wouldn't it be better to go without the sin of giving up the one true Church?

But John got what he wanted from the Union of Florence. As soon as it was signed, the pope promised military and financial help against the Turks. The Serbian capital Belgrade had fallen in 1440, so

Icon of the Virgin and Child, fifteenth or sixteenth century. This icon is based on an earlier icon from the fourteenth century. The image of the Christ child embracing the Virgin Mary was a popular one in the late Byzantine period. The Byzantine style of icon painting survived in many later Slavic and Hellenic cultures. This example is of gesso (plaster of Paris or gypsum used in painting), fabric, and paint on wood.

<small>SOURCE:</small> The Malcove Collection, University of Toronto Art Centre, Toronto, Canada.

the last Balkan power that could stand up to the Ottomans was finished. North of the Danube, the Hungarians knew they would be next. The western powers saw the dangers of letting the Turks past this natural barrier. In 1443 the Byzantines and the Hungarians attacked the Turks from the north, while to the south the Albanians revolted and the Byzantines fortified the Hexamilion, a "six-mile wall" that cut across the Isthmus of Corinth and protected the Morea, the rich province in the Peloponnese.

The campaign started well. Most of the twenty-five thousand men were Hungarian, backed by a western fleet on the Black Sea coast. The army took Serbia. Sultan Murad, fearing the loss of more territory, signed a peace treaty. But as soon as the sultan's troops moved south, the Hungarians set out again, cutting through Bulgaria.

The sultan rushed back to the scene with an army three times the size of the Hungarians' army. They met at Varna, in modern Bulgaria. The Turks marched into battle with a copy of the peace treaty fixed to their standard. They soundly defeated the Hungarians and sent them fleeing back to the Danube.

The sultan turned his wrath on the Byzantines. In 1446 he broke through the Hexamilion with artillery. Although the cannons of the time were crude, inaccurate, and slow, they proved effective against stone fortifications. He plundered the Morea and returned to his territory leading sixty thousand Greek slaves.

The Union of Florence had failed to protect Byzantium. John tried throughout his reign to convince his people it was their only hope, but to no avail. When he died in 1448, he was no closer to his goal.

VIII.

THE FALL AND AFTER

(1448–53)

⟫⋅⟪

In the year A.D. 1449, Constantine XI Palaiologos, emperor of the Romans, surveyed the lands that were now his. Taking the throne had been a long struggle; religious divisions and the ambitions of his own brothers had stood in his way. But Constantine could now say he was the ruler of an empire that was heir to centuries of civilization, God's kingdom on Earth, and Europe's bulwark against the spread of Islam.

Or so it once had been. Byzantium in 1449 was a mere ghost of the great power it had been in the Middle Ages. Its territory consisted of the city of Constantinople, a few impoverished villages and orchards surrounding it, and the Morea—a region of the southern Peloponnese dotted with monasteries and fortified towns. All of Byzantium's Asian territories were gone. Bulgaria and Thrace were now Ottoman territories. Jerusalem was long lost. The power of Orthodoxy, too, was slipping away. Its spiritual center was still Constantinople, but most of its learning and art was taking place at Mt. Athos, now in Ottoman territory, or in Russia. Some culture still flourished in the Morea, but devastating Turkish raids had nearly extinguished that too. Byzantium itself was an Ottoman vassal state. The Byzantine army, such as it was, was periodically humiliated by being obliged to fight alongside the Muslim armies against the

Christian peoples of Europe. No one fooled themselves into thinking this partnership on the field made Byzantium safe.

Constantine was the natural choice for the throne. When John VIII sailed west in search of help, he left Constantine as his regent in the capital. Constantine was almost alone in his family in being fully in support of his brother. He was uncomfortable about the Union of Florence, but he, like John, saw it as necessary for their survival.

In 1443 Constantine became the despot of Mistra, the capital of the Morea. As such he was nominally in charge of Byzantium's last province. In reality, he had to vie for control with his two brothers. Through patient leadership he was able to get the region organized enough to fortify the Hexamilion, or "six-mile wall," across the Isthmus of Corinth. Completed during the campaign of 1444, it was leveled by Turkish artillery only two years later. Constantine had to swear an oath of fealty to the sultan and pay an annual tribute. He also had to swear never to rebuild the wall. Constantine was defeated, but his fortitude must have made an impression on both the emperor and the sultan.

When news reached the Morea in 1448 that the emperor John was dead, Constantine's other two brothers raced to the capital in hopes of drumming up support. Constantine was the furthest away and knew he would never get there in time. He had to rely on John's wife Helena, now regent, to act on his behalf. She did not disappoint him. She sent representatives to Mistra to proclaim him emperor.

While their decree was legally binding, Constantine never followed the tradition of having a coronation ceremony in the Hagia Sophia, nor was he consecrated by the Orthodox patriarch or any bishop. Many Byzantines said that because of this omission he was not fully emperor. Constantine had little choice. The patriarch in Constantinople was a supporter of the Union, so getting crowned by him might undermine his popular support rather than strengthen it.

Constantine still faced strong opposition for his support of the Union. One of his most vocal critics was the monk Gennadios. Earlier in life he had been a Byzantine representative at the Council of Florence, but he changed his mind about Union and spent his days writing critiques portraying it as a craven and unholy submission to Rome.

Mistra, general view showing the fortress of the Crusader chronicler Ville-hardouin, and ruins of the upper town. Mistra was the capital of the Morea. In the Palaeologian period the Morea was a relatively wealthy region that patronized the arts.

SOURCE: Dumbarton Oaks, Byzantine Photograph and Fieldwork Archives, Washington, DC. Photograph by Cyril Mango.

In spite of such internal dissension, there was peace at first. The sultan, Murad, was an old man and was content to keep the Byzantines under his thumb as vassals. He had responded brutally when provoked by the campaign of 1444, but did not try to conquer Byzantium. But in 1451, Constantine heard troubling news. Murad had died. His nineteen-year-old son Mehmed, a warlike and zealous man, now took control.

Constantine did his best to placate Mehmed, even going so far as offering to marry Murad's widow, a Serbian noblewoman named Maria Branković. While Mehmed was the progeny of one of Murad's other wives, Constantine hoped the marriage would tie the two royal houses closer together. Mehmed didn't seem to object, but Maria would have none of it. She hated her arranged marriage to a Muslim, and swore that if he died she would never remarry. Constantine thereby lost a chance to secure his future.

At home there were other problems. The treasury was nearly empty. When Constantine tried to raise tariffs on the Venetian merchants, they threatened to move to a Turkish port. Constantine gave in. In 1451, Patriarch Gregory II resigned. He complained to the pope that the Greeks refused the Catholic services required under the Union. He soon left for Italy. The pope reiterated to Constantine that if he wanted help from the western provinces, he would have to fully enforce the Union. The pope sent one of his cardinals to Constantinople. Based in the Genoese colony of Galata, the cardinal threatened to excommunicate Byzantines who didn't honor the pope in their prayers. His proclamations caused riots, but soon the Byzantines became preoccupied with more pressing matters.

Living in Constantinople was a member of the Ottoman royal family named Orhan. He had some claim to the Ottoman throne, but Mehmed was in power and kept a sharp eye on him, not allowing him to enter Turkish territory. He sent a regular allowance to Constantine for Orhan's upkeep on the understanding that the emperor would keep Orhan quiet. Constantine sent a letter to Sultan Mehmed implying that if he didn't increase Orhan's annual subsidy, Constantine would allow Orhan to leave the city. This was a direct threat to Mehmed's right to the throne. The sultan's vizier abused Constantine's messengers, calling them stupid and saying that if the Byzantines tried anything, they would "lose what little you still have."[1]

Mehmed was good to his word. The first thing he did was to start building a castle on the European side of the Bosphorus, across from Anadolu Hisar. He called it Rumeli Hisar, "the European castle." Constantine protested, but could do nothing to stop him. The Ottomans worked fast, and in less than six months had a complete fortress on European soil. Its cannon dominated the route to the Black Sea. When it was finished in 1452, the sultan declared that all ships passing by would have to pay a toll.

---

1. Nicol, *Immortal Emperor*, p. 52. Reprinted with the permission of Cambridge University Press.

Constantine sent letters to the rulers of the western realms, begging for aid in the war that was sure to come. The Genoese and Venetians dithered. The pope had sent two hundred archers along with the cardinal. These bowmen weren't much against the full might of the Turkish army, but there was an implicit promise of more aid to come. Many Orthodox Greeks, however, were not convinced. They had no intention of subjecting their souls to the Catholic Church. There were riots in the streets, and the monk Gennadios nailed a proclamation to his door saying he preferred death over Union.

Shortly afterwards, a Venetian ship tried to go through the Bosphorus without paying the toll. The cannons at Rumeli Hisar fired on it. The ship sank and most of the crew drowned. Those who made it to shore were immediately executed.

At this point the cardinal and the emperor decided it would be a good time to have a celebration honoring the Union of Florence at the Hagia Sophia. Constantine hoped it might spur Rome into action. An unenthusiastic crowd listened to a liturgy praising the pope and the patriarch, who was still living in Italy away from his recalcitrant flock.

Constantine also made more practical plans for defense. He repaired the walls, stocked up on as much food and armaments as he could afford, and kept a steady but mostly fruitless correspondence with the western rulers. Little help came from his brothers in the Morea, who spent most of their energy disputing the boundaries of their territories. They were easy prey when Mehmed suddenly invaded late in 1452. The land was ravaged yet again. Now the Morea was too weak to come to the capital's aid even if it had wanted to.

Constantine's hope was maintained by encouraging signs from the foreigners living in Constantinople. The Venetian merchants, angered by the killing of some of their own, voted to stay and help in the defense of the city. Many of the Genoese residents did the same. Even more promisingly, a Genoese mercenary named Giovanni Giustiniani Longo showed up with seven hundred soldiers. He so impressed the emperor with his strategic planning and leadership ability that Constantine made him the commander of the entire defense. Some supply ships came in from the western provinces as well, but it seemed the emperor could expect little else.

Ironically, the man who could have given the Byzantines the most help was turned away. A Hungarian engineer named Urban had been working for the Turks for a few years. It was he who designed the cannon that had worked so well on the Venetian merchant ship. Now he came over from the Ottoman camp to offer his services in defense of the city. This initiative wasn't because he was a Christian or because he felt remorseful for helping the Turks; he was simply greedy. He expected the desperate emperor to pay any price he asked for his cannon, but Constantine had no money to spend. Once Urban realized this, he returned to Mehmed's service.

Urban set to work constructing the largest cannon the world had ever seen. More than twenty-six feet long, it could shoot a stone ball weighing twelve hundred pounds more than a mile. Dragging it into position took thirty oxen.

On April 2, 1453, the vanguard of the Turkish army arrived at the city. They set up their giant cannon and about sixty smaller artillery pieces near the thick triple set of walls on the landward side. The bombardment started almost immediately. An immense fleet appeared in the Bosphorus but, as so many times before, the Greeks put a barrier across the harbor and denied them access to the Golden Horn. On the opposite shore, the Turkish army surrounded Galata. The Genoese trading colony declared neutrality, but kept their gates locked and their walls manned just in case.

Inside the city, Constantine tried to keep the outnumbered Venetians, Genoese, and Greek defenders confident and unified—not an easy task. The two Italian city-states were longtime rivals. Moreover, the Italians were very unpopular with the Greeks. Mistrust among the men was high. Food was scarce, and people had to pay an exorbitant price for grain. Three days into the siege, three Genoese ships and a cargo vessel full of grain ran the Turkish blockade. The barrier was lifted and the ships slipped in. These ships were the last help the city would receive from the outside world.

For weeks the large cannons pounded the walls. By night the defenders rebuilt them with rubble and timber. Constantine melted down ritual objects from the churches to pay for the repairs and buy food to give to the poor. Giustiniani proved to be an able commander. He and the emperor seemingly were everywhere, overseeing the rebuilding efforts, rallying the troops, and trying to reassure the populace.

The Turks kept up a heavy bombardment and tried to storm the walls again and again, but they were pushed back each time. They even tried undermining the walls, but the defenders discovered their tunnels and dug countertunnels. A desperate underground fight ensued, with men stabbing each other in the cramped darkness. Once again the defenders pushed the Turks back. They set fire to the wooden supports and collapsed the tunnels so the Turks couldn't try this again.

Mehmed knew he needed another tactic. The cannons were doing well; there were near breaches in many spots. But the repeated assaults on these weak points were costing him time and men. There were rumors of a Venetian fleet coming to the rescue, and Mehmed needed to finish the siege before they arrived. The pope was indeed trying to send a relief fleet, but it was stalled in Italy over an argument about who would pay for the campaign. Neither Mehmed nor Constantine knew that, and both spent many anxious moments scanning the horizon.

Mehmed decided to try something that the Byzantines would never expect. On the night of April 22–23, his army laid slats on the ground and pulled about seventy ships along the relatively flat land north of Galata, over a low rise, and into the Golden Horn. When the sun rose, the residents of Constantinople saw Turkish ships in the harbor. An invading fleet had gotten into the harbor only once before, when the Crusaders attacked in 1204. The Byzantines knew very well what had happened after that.

That night the Venetians sent out their ships for a surprise attack. As they were approaching the Turkish ships, a light was seen shining from a high tower in Galata. Whether someone was warning the Turks is not clear, but by the time the Venetians made it to the Turkish fleet, it was ready to fight. The Venetian ships, badly outnumbered, were soon destroyed. The harbor was now completely in Turkish hands.

The barrier across the harbor entrance was removed and more of the fleet sailed in. Now the Turks could attack the smaller sea walls

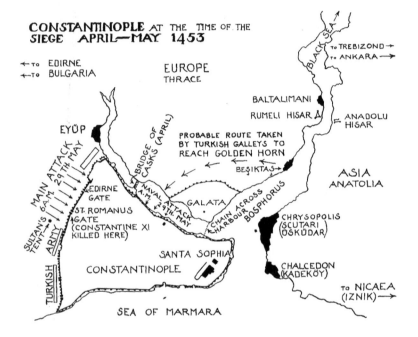

CONSTANTINOPLE AT THE TIME OF THE
SIEGE APRIL—MAY 1453

← TO EDIRNE
← TO BULGARIA

EUROPE
THRACE

← TO TREBIZOND →
← TO ANKARA →

BLACK SEA

BALTALIMANI
RUMELI HISAR

ANADOLU
HISAR

EYÜP

BRIDGE OF CASKS (APRIL)

PROBABLE ROUTE TAKEN
BY TURKISH GALLEYS TO
REACH GOLDEN HORN

BEŞIKTAS→

ASIA
ANATOLIA

MAIN ATTACK 29TH MAY

EDIRNE
GATE

ST. ROMANUS
GATE
(CONSTANTINE XI
KILLED HERE)

NAVAL ATTACK 29TH MAY

GALATA

CHAIN ACROSS HARBOUR

BOSPHORUS

CHRYSOPOLIS
(SCUTARI)
(ÜSKÜDAR)

SULTAN'S 6 A.M. TENT

TURKISH ARMY

SANTA SOPHIA

CONSTANTINOPLE

CHALCEDON
(KADEKÖY)

TO NICAEA
(IZNIK)→

SEA OF MARMARA

The siege of Constantinople, showing the route the Ottoman Turks used to bring their ships overland into the harbor.

SOURCE: *City of Constantine, 324–453,* by J.E.N. Hearsey, (John Murray Publishers, Ltd., 1963).

as well as the land walls. The defenders were already stretched thin, and they could barely hold this new front in the siege.

Constantine offered to buy Mehmed off with a lavish tribute, but the old Byzantine trick didn't work this time. The sultan was too close to winning. Instead, Mehmed offered the Greeks safe passage out of the city, saying Constantine could rule unmolested in the Morea. This was the one concession Constantine could not make. He could not abandon the capital to the infidel. He was the defender of God's kingdom on Earth. He was the rightful Christian ruler of Christ's capital city. On a more practical level, he knew that he would never be able to retake the city, nor be safe as long as Mehmed lived. Constantine replied that he would give the sultan anything he wanted but the capital. He would rather die defending it. Mehmed never sent a reply.

By late May the defenders had been under constant bombardment for more than six weeks. They were strung so thinly along the perimeter that they got little sleep, there being no men to relieve them. The breaches in the walls grew bigger, and their repair more desperate. Sensing victory was close at hand, the Turkish attacks became more determined.

The people of Constantinople turned to their religion for help. The citizenry went in a solemn procession carrying an icon of the Virgin Mary, who had protected the city for eleven hundred years. But as they went out into the streets the icon slipped from its frame. As people rushed to set it aright, they were pelted by a sudden hailstorm. The superstitious Byzantines had more to wonder about the following night. It was foggy, and as the fog dissipated in the evening, the people could see a strange glow around the base of the dome of the Hagia Sophia. The glow slowly rose to the gold cross at the summit, then winked out. The Byzantines did not know what to make of this portent. Perhaps some residual mist had caught the light of a fire or the moon (the moon was just past full that night), but to the superstitious medieval mind, especially at such a dramatic moment, the spectacle had to mean something more. The sultan's army saw it too. Mehmed was worried, but one of his advisers declared that it was the spirit of God abandoning the city.

ḥ ʌ ꞇ ι ʌ   s o p ḥ ι ʌ

A reconstruction of how the Hagia Sophia originally looked before it was turned into a mosque.

SOURCE: School of Architecture, College of Architecture, Planning, and Landscape Architecture, University of Arizona.

On May 28, there was a lull in the fighting. Mehmed declared a day of rest and prayer before the final assault. The defenders, Orthodox and Catholic alike, gathered in the Hagia Sophia to pray. Constantine spoke to his men one last time, reminding them that they were defending not only God's city, but the glory of the Roman Empire. The entire speech, the last recorded oration of the Roman world, has come down to us.

> "Gentlemen, illustrious captains of the army, and our most Christian comrades in arms: we now see the hour of battle approaching. I have therefore elected to assemble you here to make it clear that you must stand together with firmer resolution than ever. You have always fought with glory against the enemies of Christ. Now the defense of your

fatherland and of the city known the world over, which the infidel and evil Turks have been besieging for two and fifty days, is committed to your lofty spirits. Be not afraid because the walls have been worn down by the enemy's battering. For your strength lies in the protection of God and you must show it with your arms quivering and your swords brandished against the enemy. I know that this undisciplined mob will, as is their custom, rush upon you with loud cries and ceaseless volleys of arrows. These will do you no bodily harm, for I see that you are well covered in armor. They will strike the walls, our breastplates and our shields. So do not imitate the Romans who, when the Carthaginians went into battle against them, allowed their cavalry to be terrified by the fearsome sight and sound of elephants. In this battle you must stand firm and have no fear, no thought of flight, but be inspired to resist with ever more Herculean strength. Animals may run away from animals. But you are men, men of stout heart, and you will hold at bay these dumb brutes, thrusting your spears and swords into them, so that they will know that they are fighting not against their own kind but against the masters of animals.

You are aware that the impious and infidel enemy has disturbed the peace unjustly. He has violated the oath and treaty that he made with us; he has slaughtered our farmers at harvest time; he has erected a fortress on the Propontis as it were to devour the Christians; he has encircled Galata under a pretense of peace. Now he threatens to capture the city of Constantine the Great, your fatherland, the place of ready refuge for all Christians, the guardian of all Greeks, and to profane its holy shrines of God by turning them into stables for his horses. Oh my lords, my brothers, my sons, the everlasting honor of Christians is in your hands. You men of Genoa, men of courage and famous for your infinite victories, you who have always protected this city, your mother, in many a conflict with the Turks, show now your prowess and your aggressive spirit toward them with manly vigor. You men of Venice, most valiant heroes, whose swords have many a time made Turkish blood to flow and who in our time have sent so many ships, so many infidel souls to the depths under the command of Loredano, the most excellent captain of our fleet, you who have adorned this city as if it were your own with fine, outstanding men, lift high your spirits now for battle. You, my comrades in arms, obey the commands of your leaders in the knowledge that this is the day of your glory—a day on which, if you shed but a drop of blood, you will win for yourselves crowns of martyrdom and eternal fame."[2]

The next morning the final attack began. A wave of Turks flung themselves at the largest breach, screaming their battle cries. The Italians and Greeks, led by Giustiniani, fought them off. Another attack followed shortly after the first. The fight continued, more desperate than before. The defenders had no reinforcements, while the Turks could draw on almost unlimited supplies of men. Dawn turned to morning, and morning to afternoon. The defenders were tiring. Then Mehmed sent a third wave against the walls, composed of his janissary corps. The janissaries were an elite army of slaves raised from childhood in the sultan's care. They were highly trained and fanatically loyal. They swarmed into the breach, but still the Greeks and Italians held them back.

Then, just as the attack was losing momentum, Giustiniani was seriously wounded by a cannon shot. Constantine begged him to stay at his post and rally the troops, but his men carried him away. Seeing Giustiniani withdraw, the defenders began to lose heart. Men started slipping to the rear. The janissaries made a final assault and broke through the breach. The inner wall still had its gate open, and the defenders now fled through it in a disorganized mass. Constantine tried to stem the tide, or at least get them to close that final gate, but to no avail. Seeing all was lost, Constantine flung aside his imperial regalia and charged into the fray. He died fighting.

---

2. Nicol, *Immortal Emperor,* pp. 68–69, reprinted with the permission of Cambridge University Press.

Historians have long wondered why Constantine chose to die that day, and why he did not accept Mehmed's offer of safe passage. Perhaps he did not want to be remembered as a coward. Perhaps he knew he would never be safe as Mehmed's vassal. Perhaps, too, he hoped that if he showed courage at the end, Byzantium would be remembered for its glory days and its principles, and not as the broken-down vassal state it had become. We will never know the answer, but on that day his legend was born.

The rest of the battle was over quickly. As Ottoman troops fought their way into the city, Greeks and Italians fled to the port to escape on the few ships left to them. Most were able to slip past the Turkish fleet and head for the nearest friendly harbor. Mehmed allowed his soldiers free rein for three days, the traditional punishment for a city that resisted siege. Many homes were burned, including the Jewish quarter, and tens of thousands of Byzantines were led away in slavery. The Byzantines locked themselves in the Hagia Sophia and started a final Mass to plead to God and the Virgin Mary. They never got to finish it. The Turks burst in and cut them down. Legend says the priest walked through a door in the wall and sealed himself in, only to return and finish the Mass when Constantinople is once again the capital of Byzantium. Another legend, told in Greece to this day, says that Constantine was carried away by angels and sealed beneath the earth. Like King Arthur, he is not dead, but only sleeping, and will one day rise up and retake his city.

The Byzantine Empire was no more. The Morea, now a province without a capital, held on for a few more years, but in 1460 Sultan Mehmed conquered it, too. Trebizond, an independent Byzantine kingdom since the Fourth Crusade, fell the next year.

But empires do not truly fall. The government was gone, the last emperor dead without an heir, but the way of life continued. Mehmed was eager to rebuild Constantinople as his own capital. He turned the Hagia Sophia into a mosque, but he allowed many other Orthodox churches to remain open. He appointed Gennadios, the monk who so vehemently opposed the Union of Florence, to be the new Orthodox patriarch. Now that the reason to unify with Rome was gone, Gennadios was able to maintain an independent Orthodox

Church under Ottoman rule. In 1472, the leaders of the Orthodox Church met and declared the Union of Florence null and void. Mehmed also offered property in the city at a reduced price to encourage people to settle there. Turks came in large numbers, but so did Greeks. He gave the Genoese in Galata rights to trade in Constantinople as a reward for their neutrality. Business would continue as usual, but now it was under the control of the Turks. In the city, life went on. The Turks continued to spread through Europe, pushing north and west until they were finally stopped at Vienna in 1683.

The Byzantine way of life and the religious power of the Orthodox Church held sway over millions of eastern Christians long after Byzantium was only a memory. In Romania and Russia, Moldavia and Armenia, icons were still painted in the Byzantine style. Even the Turks learned from their former foes. Ottoman mosques were built with domes imitating the Hagia Sophia.

The Orthodox rite was still performed as it had been in the glory years of the empire. Romanian voivods (lords) and Russian czars used the imperial symbol of the double-headed eagle as their crest. They continued the Orthodox rites and, in their own way, held themselves up as the new emperors of the Romans. "Eastern" Europe, Christian but separate from the West, is a Byzantine legacy that is still with us today.

Italy was one of the great beneficiaries of the Byzantine civilization. The money from its trading colonies funded the Italian Renaissance. Byzantine scholars helped too. Greek refugees had been flooding into Italy for a century. Their classical learning and knowledge of Greek became in high demand as Italy underwent the first flowerings of the Renaissance. As Europe shucked off the religious strictures of medieval theology and conservatism, there was a new interest in classical thought. The Byzantines were in great demand for their classical learning and their intellectual freedom unfettered by western tradition. Just when the West was hungering to know more about the great civilizations of ancient Greece and Rome, the Byzantines began translating nearly forgotten works from Greek into Latin. For western scholars hampered by the dry scholasticism of the Middle Ages, which emphasized received wisdom over innovation,

Icon of Christ Pantokrator, seventeenth century. This popular image from the Byzantine period appears here, two centuries after the fall of Constantinople. This icon is gesso (plaster of Paris or gypsum used in painting) and paint on wood.

SOURCE: The Malcove Collection, University of Toronto Art Centre, Toronto, Canada.

Leaf from a post-Byzantine Gospel lectionary, dated to Moscow in 1596. Lectionaries are collections of quotes from the Scriptures that are read at services. This page begins a sampling of passages from the Gospel of Luke. The winged lion is the symbol of the evangelist. He is framed by a series of decorated roundels showing Christ flanked by the Virgin Mary and John the Baptist, the four evangelists, and two saints. Despite being made in Russia 150 years after the fall of Constantinople, it is greatly influenced by Byzantine manuscript painting. The lectionary was commissioned by Tsar Fedor, son of Ivan the Terrible, and given to the monastery of St. Saba near Jerusalem.

SOURCE: The Malcove Collection, University of Toronto Art Centre, Toronto, Canada.

Icon of John the Baptist, sixteenth century. Although from post-Byzantine Greece, this icon shows the survival of the late Byzantine style. It is of gesso (plaster of Paris or gypsum used in painting), paint, and gold leaf on wood.

this was like the opening of a whole new world. Many plays, speeches, philosophies, and scientific efforts of the classical world became available in the West for the first time since the barbarian invasions a thousand years before. The modern concepts of science and the arts that come from the Renaissance were inspired in part by the last empire of Rome.

IX.

Daily Life

———⊰◆⊱———

The Imperial Family

Byzantium went through several dynasties. Their founders were often men of humble origin, usually soldiers who rose through the ranks to positions of influence. Other dynasties were created by important and wealthy families. Even after a dynasty was overthrown, these families would often retain positions of power. Thus in the Palaiologan period, members of the Doukas and Komnenos families still owned large estates and held positions in government.

The emperor was the center of an elaborate ritual of pomp and ceremony. He was constantly surrounded by courtiers and ministers. His job was often shared with one or more co-emperors. After the dissolution of the western empire in the fifth century, these co-emperors did not rule any actual land. Instead, they held various governmental duties. Often an emperor would name one of his sons co-emperor in order to secure his succession. At other times, a powerful faction at court would force the emperor to name a co-emperor, who then would dominate the throne.

It is not surprising, then, that succession was a complicated and often bloody process. If the emperor died without a grown child, the empress often would take over as regent. While some remarkable women such as Zoe held onto power, the empress would usually

171

choose a successor from among the various candidates. At times the empress would marry the new emperor in order to keep her position.

Just as there could be more than one emperor, there could be two or more empresses. The emperor named the empress, and while he usually would name his wife, the title was not automatic. At times the emperor would name a female relative to be empress in addition to or instead of his wife.

In theory, an emperor had to be approved by three factions: the Senate, the army, and the people. The army was usually the deciding factor, but many emperors found to their regret that the people would quickly shift their loyalties to another contender if they were unhappy. The Senate was less powerful as an entity than it was as a mouthpiece for the views of many of the leading families.

While the emperor had to please all these factions and stay within the good graces of the Church, he wielded a great deal of power. He was the final word on all laws, foreign and religious policy. He was the pinnacle of the army, the Church and the bureaucracy. Considering the elaborate administration that ran all these organizations, the rulers of Byzantium had far more control over the workings of their empire than the kings of western Europe. Western kings had to deal with independent-minded feudal lords, the spiritual authority of the pope, and their own limited governmental apparatus. A complex state government such as that of the Byzantines would not be found in western Europe until the Renaissance.

The Poor

In all societies, the great bulk of the population is made up of the poor and powerless. For them, the lives of kings and nobility are rarely seen, glimpsed from a distance or not at all. The theories and innovations of the clergy and scholars mean little to them. Life for the poor is one of ceaseless toil, unrewarding work, and the constant threat of want.

Byzantine civilization was no exception. Poverty was a chronic problem, especially in the capital and other large cities, but Byzan-

PLATE 8
BYZANTINE EMPIRE

Page   Emperor   Servant girl   Empress and princess

Nineteenth-century rendering of the Byzantine imperial costume.
SOURCE: *Historic Costume in Pictures*, by Braun & Schneider (Dover Publications, Inc., 1975).

tium was ahead of its time in caring for the needy. There was a well-organized system of charity that cared for the sick, the homeless, the aged, and the infirm. It provided food, clothing, shelter, and the chance to work. Many charitable institutions were run by churches or monasteries, but others were organized by the lay elite. The empress Theodora established a home for reformed prostitutes. The emperor Alexios I set up an entire neighborhood in Constantinople where those in need could find care and shelter.

There were also emergencies to be dealt with. Wars and earthquakes could leave entire populations indigent. The Church gained much of its early popularity by responding to these crises more quickly and efficiently than the government.

Still, this well-organized system could not deal with all those who needed help, just as modern societies fail to do so today. Beggars were common. The streets rang with their cry of "Give us your small change of silver and bronze to buy our daily bread. Everyone says that starving to death is the worst way to go."[1] The blind and the lame sat on corners in the hope of a handout, while prostitutes stood nearby, hoping to earn enough for their next meal.

In the countryside the situation was not much different. Many farmers did not own their land, or were in such debt to their wealthy neighbors that they were in constant danger of losing it. A single bad crop was often enough to bankrupt poorer families, while the rural aristocracy snapped up their land at a bargain price. Emperors sometimes forcibly gave the land back in order to reduce the power of the rural elite, but this confiscation was only the restarting of a cycle, not a permanent solution.

During bad years the rural poor often flocked to cities in the hope of finding work. They rarely did. The massive number of poor people in cities such as Constantinople and Nicaea was a constant problem. Some emperors put them to work on public projects such as building churches or repairing city walls, but such measures were never enough. One of the reasons monasteries grew so large was the number of poor taking vows. The monk's life was a hard one of constant prayer and labor, but at least it guaranteed bread.

Despite the wide difference in wealth between the poor and those in power, there was little organized rebellion. Constantinople saw numerous riots during which the mob ransacked houses of the rich. When there was an attempted coup, both sides would encourage the looting of the other's property. But these riots were mere opportunism, not organized revolt. The only uprising that comes close to the modern idea of a class revolution was the Zealot outbreak of the 1340s. This uprising seems to have been a true attempt at changing the social order by striking against the rich and powerful as a group, but it is difficult to tell what its exact ideology was. Sadly, the only

---

1. Cavallo, "Introduction," p. 5. Used by permission of the University of Chicago Press. © 1997 the University of Chicago.

surviving records of the revolt were written by its enemies, and they reveal little of the motivations of the Zealots.

As with other societies, the poor accepted their lot with little complaint. The Church gave spiritual comfort and some material aid, but in general the poor suffered in silence, and their stories went unrecorded.

Farmers

Like all preindustrial societies, the Byzantine Empire was predominantly rural. The vast majority of people lived simple lives, tending flocks and tilling the soil. Unlike in the West, where the development of the feudal system led to a gradual constriction of farmers' rights and their ability to own land, there were large numbers of freeholders in many periods of Byzantine history. However, economic pressures such as high taxes, which were paid disproportionately by the poor, often led to bankruptcy and the loss of land to owners of large estates. In some periods these rural manors grew so large they almost became autonomous states. They had their own peasantry, fortifications, soldiers, and even currency. Periodically, emperors would forcibly redistribute the land, so the Byzantine countryside went through cycles of centralization and decentralization.

The basis of country life was the village. Villages could range in size from a few houses to several hundred families complete with defenses, a church, and sometimes a local monastery. Houses were small, one or two rooms, with the largest room having a hearth. They were made of whatever materials were easily available. In the rugged terrain of Greece that material was stone. In Egypt it was reeds. The economy of the village varied depending on the region. In Egypt and Asia Minor, the crop was predominantly grain. Greece and the Levant supported herds of sheep and goats. Shorelines were dotted with fishing villages, many quite large. One record tells of an inland village supporting itself with artificial fishponds.[2] These early commercial fishermen paid the bulk of their taxes in fish.

2. Kazhdan, "The Peasantry," p. 55.

Food was fairly diverse. Bread made up the bulk of the diet. Beans, fruit, dairy products, and eggs were important, as were olives in some areas. The temperate Mediterranean climate made it possible to grow winter crops in many areas. Vineyards produced wine. Asia Minor had large areas for grazing, and the flocks of sheep, pigs and cattle probably outnumbered people. Even so, meat was expensive and not eaten frequently by the common folk. Animals were generally too valuable to slaughter. Many monks were vegetarians, their monastic rules forbidding meat or limiting it to important holidays as a way to avoid worldly excess.

Villages were mostly self-sufficient. Hand mills and watermills ground grain, olive presses made olive oil, and wool and flax were processed to make clothing. Beehives produced honey. This was the best natural source of sugar and was in high demand at the Byzantine table. Honey had to be imported from Russia to meet with demand. Bees also produced wax for candles, important for lighting as well as for church services. The oil lamp, so common in Roman times, gradually fell out of favor both in Byzantium and in western Europe.

Clothing was made of wool or linen. Only the upper classes could afford the brocaded silks for which Byzantine weavers were famous. After the early centuries men traded in the old Roman tunic, basically a long shirt that hung down to just above the knees, for trousers, shirts, and cloaks. Women covered their hair and wore long tunics that reached down to their ankles.

Land was plowed using mules and donkeys. Horses were rare and expensive in Byzantium and mostly used by the army and the nobility. When Basil made his epic gallop across the empire, his soldiers had to settle for riding mules because there weren't enough horses available.

While the history of Byzantium is filled with violent raids that destroyed the countryside, most villages did not experience war on a regular basis. When the weather was good, village life was much more bearable than the cramped, uncertain, and unsanitary life in the cities. There were frequent saint's days, many with pagan roots, to give some time for revelry and feasting.

Bronze lamp in the form of a peacock, sixth century. Oil lamps were the main method of interior lighting in the early centuries of Byzantium. In later centuries they would gradually be replaced by candles. Common people used ceramic oil lamps, while the well-to-do used lamps made of metal. Lamps came in an endless variety of shapes and styles. This example was found in Egypt, where peacock lamps seemed to have been especially popular. To the left is a bronze lamp handle of the same period, decorated with a cross, acanthus leaves, and a pair of panthers.
SOURCE: The Malcove Collection, University of Toronto Art Centre, Toronto, Canada.

Discord in the village was kept to a minimum through detailed laws on the sharing of resources. A villager could collect wood on his neighbor's land, or fish from his pond. He was allowed to eat grapes from his neighbor's vineyard, but couldn't take any away to sell. This system provided relief for the poor and encouraged a feeling of mutual dependence.

The farmer's biggest fear was not of the invader, but of the tax collector. Much business was done in cash; small denomination coins of silver and bronze were common. Western feudal Europe was mostly an in-kind economy, but the Byzantines were expected to pay their taxes in coin. Taxes were always high, at times ruinously so, and tax collectors were authorized to get the money by whatever means they thought necessary. Farmers who couldn't pay were often beaten or tied to trees and set upon by starving dogs. Farmers would often resort to moneylenders for relief, but a series of bad years often meant foreclosure on their land.

Women

The role of women in Byzantine society was a complex one. Their opportunities for work and positions of influence were severely limited, but historical records are filled with exceptions to this rule. Women were considered spiritually weak, the receptacles of evil and temptation. They were blamed for Man's downfall from the Garden of Eden. On the other hand, female saints and the Virgin Mary were held up as exemplars of piety and holiness. For most women, however, their influence was in the home, where they had a great deal of say over family affairs and the running of the household.

Separation of the sexes was a hallmark of Byzantine society, and the division began at birth. Girls were weaned earlier than boys and fed less. Female infanticide was sometimes practiced, even though both Church and civil law forbade it. Girls were cloistered in the home from a very young age. In *Digenis Akritis*, a twelfth century epic, the hero woos a beautiful girl away from her protective household. While she eventually obliges him, she proudly proclaims,

> "I never put my head out the window. I kept myself unseen by others. Apart from my kinsmen and a few close friends, no one ever saw the features of my face as I observed carefully the role that is appropriate to unmarried girls. I have gone beyond these bounds and I have broken the rules and I have become shameless for love of you."[3]

---

3. Jeffreys, *Digenis Akritis*, p. 97. Reprinted with the permission of Cambridge University Press.

This author wasn't taking artistic license to emphasize the ideal of chastity. Unmarried women, especially of the wealthier classes, spent little time outside the home. When they did, they were escorted by male relatives, older women, or servants. One acceptable outing for women was church, and they flocked to it in great numbers. But even here women sat separately from men, often in a balcony to the rear behind screens of silk. Another place they could go were the public baths, which had special days during the week for women. In modern Turkey there are many baths that still do this.

Women wore long-sleeved tunics that covered them from the neck down to their feet. Their hair was covered. Despite such modesty, clothes were often sumptuous, with gold brocade and heavy jewelry for those who could afford it. Cosmetics were used to whiten the skin and redden the cheeks and lips. Priests criticized women for showing off their finery in church, but it seemed to do little good.

Few girls received any formal education. Some nunneries had schools for girls, and wealthier families often hired a tutor, but in general a girl's education involved helping her mother. Sewing, weaving, and brocading were considered especially important skills, and silk-weaving was one of the few high-paying jobs open to women. Byzantine writers would often compliment a woman by describing how well she made clothes.

Both women and men married young, usually in their early to mid-teens. For the sake of a good match, girls were sometimes married off as young as five years old. When parents were looking for a spouse for their child, the main thing they looked at was the status of the other family. Marriage was a unification of two families, so land, businesses, and titles all had to be taken into account. For a woman past puberty not to be married was considered wasteful.

Once the parents of the girl found a suitable man, the family of the groom-to-be would give the girl's family an expensive gift that would act as a contract. If the boy's family broke off the engagement, the girl's family got to keep the gift. If the girl's family broke it off, they had to return the gift and a sum equal to its value. The bride also received a dowry from her parents, to which she retained the rights for the rest of her life.

Detail from a gold marriage belt, Constantinople, sixth or seventh century. A belt such as this would be given by the groom to the bride on their wedding night. The scene shows the joining of the couple's right hands together, a rite still performed in Orthodox weddings. This symbolizes the couple becoming as one, joined by Jesus in holy matrimony.

SOURCE: Dumbarton Oaks, Byzantine Photograph and Fieldwork Archives, Washington, DC.

On the wedding day, the bride would bathe and don a white dress or robe. She would then go to church, where she joined the groom. A priest placed crowns on the couple's heads, at which point they exchanged rings and shared a cup of wine. Following the ceremony, the couple would parade back to the groom's house while wellwishers followed them singing songs. At the home they would preside over a large feast, during which they would slip away to the bedroom. There the groom presented the bride with a marriage belt, and they consummated the union.

Couples would have many children. Women could expect to be pregnant or nursing for most of their fertile years. Some birth control existed in the form of herbal concoctions that acted as spermicides, but since they were a favorite tool of the prostitutes they were considered shameful. How many women used them is unknown, since married women rarely admitted to it. This was a very sensitive subject for a prudish society, so it is not surprising that there is little discussion of it in Byzantine texts, the vast majority of which were written by men.

Abortion, however, was widely discussed. Abortion was legal in cases where the mother's life was at risk. Physicians performed it frequently—so frequently, in fact, that one has to wonder how in danger some of the women were. Abortion in other cases was illegal and subject to severe punishment.

Once married, a woman's life was much like it was before, only now she cared for her husband and children instead of her male relatives and younger siblings. Women generally did not have jobs outside the home, although they often helped in their husband's farm or business. Poorer women might work as maids or cooks for a richer family. Women sometimes ran their own shops, and a few professions, such as midwifery and matchmaking, were exclusively for women.

Another option was the nunnery. Poor families sometimes gave unwanted girls away to be raised as nuns, but more often adult women took vows. Some were fleeing the prospect of an unpleasant marriage or were escaping an abusive husband. Others took vows with their family's consent. Life in a nunnery was hard, but women were given a chance at an education and charitable, rewarding work. Monks vastly outnumbered nuns, but the nunnery was always an option for those looking for a socially acceptable alternative to marriage.

Women had little power outside the home. They could own property, but their voices held little legal weight. Only empresses and abbesses had any direct influence on politics. The one exception was in religious assembly. Since the church was one of the only places women could go without dispute or censure, it is not surprising that women spent much time there and took on important roles in the Church's charitable institutions and worship. They were especially central in the veneration of icons and saints' relics. Nuns and empresses were important supporters of the right to venerate icons during the iconoclastic controversy.

Businessmen and Trade

The Byzantine Empire went through two major phases of economy. In the early centuries, until the loss of eastern Asia Minor to the Turks after the Battle of Manzikert in 1071, Byzantium had the most advanced economy in the region. Trade flourished. As large-scale commerce collapsed in the west during the fifth and sixth centuries, the wealth of the empire shifted eastwards. The upper classes migrated to Constantinople in large numbers, as the capital offered stability and opportunity. As the eastern empire stabilized itself and expanded outwards, it took on an increasingly dominant role in the region's trade. There would be occasional crises, especially the wars with Persia, but commerce would always resume after the fighting had stopped.

Byzantium had lucrative trade with all its neighbors, and trade routes extended as far east as China. Constantinople, standing at the crossroads of Europe and Asia, became the natural focal point for commerce.

The Silk Route brought raw silk from China, which Byzantine factories skillfully wove or brocaded into beautiful garments that were the height of fashion throughout the Mediterranean and beyond. These silk clothes were the empire's main luxury export, and brought in a large amount of gold each year. When the Byzantines obtained silkworms from China, the ability to produce silk of their own drastically cut their overhead and profits skyrocketed.

Other goods traveled along the Silk Route. Some manufactured goods from China and India made it to Byzantium, as well as spices (such as pepper and cloves), herbs, and sandalwood from India. The spices were especially important. In the days before refrigeration, they helped preserve food or make it more palatable once it had become slightly spoiled. Expensive spices also became a sign of status, since only the wealthy could afford to use them. In later centuries the Mongols brought grain, furs, and slaves to Byzantium. Jewels came from Sri Lanka. All of these goods continued to be traded along the Silk Route long after domestic production dried up the demand for Chinese silk.

The easiest route ran right through Persia, but this one was periodically disrupted by war. Another route, through the nomadic lands north of the Black Sea, was equally unreliable. The southern route was by water, through the Red Sea and Egypt. This one was more stable, but subject to duty and occasional blockade by the Arabs. At no time was the route to the Far East entirely secure, and many of Byzantium's wars can be seen as attempts to secure the empire's economic lifeline, although they tended to hurt rather than help the economy.

In return for Byzantium's famous silks and trusted coinage, the empire's neighbors exchanged various commodities. Russia exported a steady supply of furs, slaves, and honey. From the Baltic region came amber. The Vikings in Scandinavia regularly sailed the rivers through Russia all the way to Constantinople in order to trade rare furs and narwhal ivory for the silks and gold of Byzantium. Some stayed and joined the Varangian Guard. The Balkans provided a great deal of raw material and slaves.

Egypt remained the biggest exporter of grain in the Mediterranean, but after it fell to the Arabs, Byzantium could no longer rely upon it for a steady supply. The Arabs exported high quality weapons, which were highly prized by the Byzantine army.

Until the ascent of the Italian city-states in the thirteenth century, Byzantium had the most advanced economy of Europe. It had much more of a cash economy than in the west. Most salaries were paid in coin, and coinage was in common use at all levels of society. Bronze was elevated to the status of a semiprecious metal so the government could issue large numbers of small-denomination coins.

International trade was either by barter or by large-denomination gold and silver coins. The nosmismus (called the solidus in Latin) was a gold coin set by Constantine at one seventy-second of a pound

Solidus of Justinian, 545–65. The solidus was a gold coin weighing 1/72 of a pound. Its weight stayed constant until the eleventh century, when the disaster at Manzikert permanently affected the Byzantine economy. The solidus was such a respected currency that it was the international medium of exchange as far away as Sri Lanka.

SOURCE: Museum of Art and Archaeology, University of Missouri-Columbia.

of gold. From the days of Constantine to the disaster at Manzikert in 1071, it was the reliable standard for much of the world. From Italy to Sri Lanka, it was valued over all other coinage. It wasn't debased until the reign of Nikephoros III (1078–81), after the loss of Anatolia to the Turks left the Byzantine economy in shambles. With the disappearance of this vital province's revenue, there was a shortage of gold, so the nosmismus was diluted with silver. Before this, Byzantine currency had more influence in the early Middle Ages than the dollar does today, often being the only trusted hard currency. After the empire allowed the Venetians and Genoese to dominate its international trade, people became more interested in Italian currency than the nosmismus.

This complex and dynamic economy was run by a powerful bureaucracy that was efficient and mostly incorruptible. A large number of functionaries checked weights and measures, collected tariffs, and regulated imports and exports.

Bronze weight with monogram, fifth to sixth century. Weights were often signed with the initials of their owners, usually merchants or government officials.

Government bureaucrats set price controls on many products by limiting the profit margin to 4–16 percent depending on the merchandise. There were limits on interest rates as well. Thus the Byzantine government had far more control over the economy than the rulers of any other country of its day. The administration knew every item that went in and out of the empire and was able to respond to shortages and gluts on the market with remarkable efficiency.

Some goods were a state monopoly. Silk, the most valuable of Byzantine exports, was closely regulated and could only be sold by the government. At first all silk came across the Silk Road from Asia, and private imports were banned. This trade was disrupted by the Persian wars, but the situation was saved when two monks smuggled some silk worms into Byzantium, hidden in hollowed-out staves. From then on the Byzantines were able to produce their own silk in large government factories. Other important goods were also government monopolies. Weapons and precious metals were all the domain of the government. Bread production was controlled by the government until Heraklios abolished the public bread dole.

Byzantine culture inherited the Roman stigma against business. Respectable families made their income from land, not trade. Businessmen were not allowed to hold aristocratic titles or to be members of the Senate. Caps on interest rates also limited their income. While some merchants became quite wealthy, the richest families were still members of the landed aristocracy.

Merchants were required to be members of a guild. Thus a man who sold furs had to be in the fur-sellers guild. Guild members were not allowed to compete with each other; they had to buy into a venture as a group, dividing the profits among themselves in proportion to their individual investments.

Beneath these early venture capitalists were the shopkeepers, small-time businessmen who rarely owned their own shops and had to rent from landlords. They sold a wide variety of goods made locally or purchased from importers. There were also peddlers who sold items such as fish and fruit on the street.

Another type of businessman was the artisan. These craftsmen were responsible for the empire's artistic heritage. They built the

Gold signet ring from the sixth or seventh century. These rings were pressed into hot wax seals in order to leave the signature of the owner.

Pair of gold earrings, tenth century or later. Note the tiny gold beads that make up most of the decoration. The difficult process of crafting these was a Byzantine specialty.

SOURCE: Museum of Art and Archaeology, University of Missouri-Columbia.

Bronze lamp in the form of a foot, fifth or sixth century. Byzantine artisans were not without a sense of humor, but they always remembered their Christianity. On the hinged conical cover at the top, used to refill the lamp, there is a cross and a palm branch.

SOURCE: The Malcove Collection, University of Toronto Art Centre, Toronto, Canada.

churches and crafted the jewelry, carved the ivory diptychs and minted the coins, yet little is known about these people. Although paid well, they were considered common laborers. Their names were rarely recorded. Unlike the masters of the Italian Renaissance, the names of the great artists of Byzantium are mostly lost to us.

The economy began to change with the reversals of the eleventh century. The loss of Asia Minor deprived Byzantium of its richest land and hampered trade with the Far East. The second crushing blow was the Fourth Crusade and the fifty years of Latin occupation that followed it. This loss of home rule seriously undermined Byzantine confidence. The capital was destroyed and impoverished, permanently decentralizing the economy. Desperate for naval support, the Palaiologoi gave concessions to the Italians. The economy became increasingly dependent on the Italian city-states for its external trade. Venice and Genoa took over much of this trade and were granted generous tax shelters.

After the Crusade, the second phase of the Byzantine economy began. Although at times it could still make its presence felt, it underwent a long, slow constriction until it was at the economic mercy of the Italians and the military mercy of the Ottomans.

Native merchants found they couldn't compete and had to satisfy themselves with internal trade. The only Greeks with the money to contest the Italians were members of the landed aristocracy. Seeing their lands shrinking and periodically destroyed by Serbian and Turkish raids, they forgot their previous reluctance and started investing in Italian ventures. This alliance helped the local economy somewhat, but not enough to reverse Byzantium's gradual slide to destruction.

The Clergy

Religion touched every part of Byzantine life. The average Byzantine thought that by maintaining strict Orthodoxy and committing no grievous sin, a place in heaven was assured. This belief explains the Byzantine obsession with fine points of doctrine and their refusal to give up their Church even when it would have been politically expedient to do so. The Orthodox Church was remarkably perseverant. After the seventh ecumenical council in 787, there were no major changes or innovations in doctrine. The Scriptures and these seven councils were, and still are, the basis of Orthodox belief.

Religious and secular life were inseparable, since Byzantines looked at everything from a religious perspective. The clergy not only presided over important events such as births, weddings, and funerals, but they also blessed new homes, prayed for fishing boats as they set sail, and blessed soldiers on their way to battle.

Commoners could be involved in their church in more ways than merely attending Mass. Many people, especially widows, went to church every day. There were a large number of religious tasks for which people could volunteer, such as working in religious charities or maintaining church buildings and lands. Pilgrimages were popular. There were day trips to local shrines and long voyages to Constantinople or Jerusalem.

Icons were revered and hung in many homes. Some icons were considered especially powerful. The historian Psellus tells us that the empress Zoe had a beloved icon of Christ that she claimed could predict the future. She would stare at it and the colors would change before her eyes. Each hue had a different meaning. There were public icons as well. Romanos III carried a special icon into battle to protect his troops. When Constantinople was attacked, the patriarch would lead a procession around the city walls, carrying an image of the Virgin Mary.

Besides offering salvation, the Church was the major philanthropy of the empire. It provided food, shelter, and money to those in need. Clergy were encouraged to be socially active. There are many stories of ideal clergymen who spent their days helping the poor. The best of these were elevated to sainthood. In one story, John, patriarch of Alexandria, was given a luxurious quilt by a wealthy parishioner. The first night he used it he couldn't fall asleep, thinking "how many are there at this minute who are grinding their teeth because of the cold?"[4] The next day he sold the quilt and used the money to buy 144 blankets that he gave out to the poor.

---

4. Rice, *Everyday Life in Byzantium*, p. 72.

Soldier and chancellor   Deacon   Bishop   Levite

Nineteenth-century rendering of Byzantine secular and religious costume.
SOURCE: *Historic Costume in Pictures*, by Braun & Schneider (Dover Publications, Inc., 1975).

Ampulla, or pilgrim flask, of St. Menas, 610–40. This saint was reputedly a camel driver before becoming a Roman soldier and then a Christian. He was martyred around 300 for preaching at a pagan festival. These pilgrim flasks were bought as mementos by visitors to saints' shrines.
SOURCE: Museum of Art and Archaeology, University of Missouri-Columbia.

Despite its central role in Byzantine life, the Church always remained subservient to the state. The emperor was the nominal head of the Church; in the Hagia Sophia his throne stood next to the patriarch's. He took an active part in services on Christmas, Palm Sunday, and other important holidays, and was the final authority at ecumenical councils. The state was never at the mercy of the Church as it was in the West. For this reason, the Byzantine aristocracy could not accept union with Rome. Not only were there religious objections, but they found the political implications of Papal supremacy unacceptable.

For all his power over the Church, the emperor rarely interfered in religious policy. The system functioned best when church and state kept to their respective spheres of influence. Clergy were not allowed to hold positions in the military or government, and those who became involved in politics lost their jobs and sometimes their lives. This system was often in the emperor's best interest, and worked well most of the time. Neither the Church nor the state approved of heresies such as the ones embraced by the Paulicians and the Bogomils, who preached disobedience to the state and a renunciation of all worldly interests.

The Church was democratic and highly organized. The patriarchs were elected by the bishops with the approval of the emperor. Originally there were five patriarchates: Rome, Constantinople, Antioch, Jerusalem, and Alexandria. Constantinople was the most powerful after the rift with Rome, and the loss of Jerusalem and Alexandria only strengthened its position.

Bishops ruled over large cities and provincial centers. They were elected by the local clergy. Bishops were required to be educated, to know the Psalter by heart, and to have lived as a monk for at least part of their lives.

Local clergy were from all levels of society. Many had little education, especially the village "popes" who, unlike popes in the west, were the most humble of the religious functionaries. These local clergy were allowed to marry, a practice still followed in the Orthodox Church.

As in political and economic life, the Byzantine flair for micro-management was applied to religious affairs as well. The patriarchs kept themselves well-informed of all aspects of their Church, and many letters survive from patriarchs to very lowly members of the clergy correcting minor points of liturgy or clarifying tricky aspects of doctrine.

Monasteries grew in importance throughout Byzantine history. They offered both security and salvation, and attracted people from all walks of life. Many people would take monastic vows in their old age, and some rich landowners built monasteries on their estates for this purpose. Monks lived a communal life, praying and working together. Donating land or money to monasteries was considered an act of good faith, and some institutions became quite rich. Emperors occasionally tried to curb their wealth and local influence, but they never succeeded for long.

Some monks preferred a more isolated life. In the early days of the Church, Syria became famous for its stylites and wandering ascetics, and some monks lived in caves or tiny houses, rarely seeing their brethren or outsiders. Others were more worldly, and the patriarch often had to remonstrate with monks who came to Constantinople on the excuse of visiting him, but really to see the sights.

At large churches, the vestments and church ornaments were very elaborate. Clerical garments were adapted from the old Roman toga and were richly brocaded. Wealthy churches were equipped with gold altars and bejeweled reliquaries. Gold or brass candlesticks and censers were used during Mass. In times of emergency, emperors would melt down some of these objects to pay the army, but someone would always donate new ones.

In the Middle Ages, Orthodox Christianity had a strong mystical streak. Individual revelations and visions were tolerated as long as they did not contradict established doctrine. This mysticism had a more exotic side as well. Survivals from pagan times were hard to suppress, especially in rural areas. Local priests and village popes complained that harvest festivals resembled Bacchic orgies, and holy wells that survived from classical times had Christian stories grafted

Pair of book covers from the Sion Treasure, silver repoussé with gilding, Constantinople, mid-sixth century. The Roman empire used scrolls for much of its history, but books replaced them by the fourth century. Since books were valuable objects, and often had religious significance as well, it is no surprise that they often came with richly decorated covers. These particular examples come from a hoard found in central Asia Minor, modern Turkey. The inscriptions state that they were commissioned by the bishop Eutychianos, and they call on "Holy Sion," which may indicate that they were the property of a local monastery founded by Nicholas of Sion.

SOURCE: Dumbarton Oaks, Byzantine Photograph and Fieldwork Archives, Washington, DC.

Silver paten showing the Communion of the Apostles, Constantinople, 565– 578. Patens are plates used to hold the eucharist bread or wafer during mass. They were often made of valuable materials. This one was found in a cache with several other pieces of church art, hidden in a time of danger and never recovered. All silver and gold in the empire was marked with an imperial stamp guaranteeing quality and weight. This piece bears the mark of Justin II (565–78). The design is of the Divine Liturgy in which Christ, shown twice, serves the bread and wine of the eucharist to the twelve apostles.

SOURCE: Dumbarton Oaks, Byzantine Photograph and Fieldwork Archives, Washington, DC.

onto the original legends. Fortunetellers and astrologers found ready customers. Even the highly educated would cast spells to win a lover or hurt an enemy.

Outsiders

In every society there are some groups that, for various reasons, do not fit in. Unlike our own culture, race and ethnicity did not matter to the Byzantines so much as religion. Those who did not subscribe to the Orthodox creed found themselves strangers in their own land. The largest religious minority in the empire was the Jews, who made up an estimated 1 percent of the population. In cities with large Jewish populations, they were segregated into their own neighborhoods. Jews were forbidden to marry Christians or hold positions in the government or military. The Jewish quarter in Constantinople was right next to where the tanners lived, and the tanners delighted in pouring the foul-smelling waste products of their industry onto the Jewish streets.

While they were second-class citizens, the Jews had a far more secure place than they did in the western kingdoms. Violent persecutions were relatively rare. Jews were respected as physicians and scholars, especially for their knowledge of Arabic texts, and were usually left in peace.

Muslims enjoyed a similar status. While they were never trusted, there was always a small Muslim community in Byzantium. Constantinople got its first mosque in 717, and another was built by John II Komnenos (1118–43) to celebrate his peace treaty with the Seljuks. Like the Jews, they were mistrusted for their faith but respected for their learning. Byzantine and Islamic scholars traded ideas and manuscripts, expanding the knowledge of both cultures. Muslim merchants were a common sight on the streets, and there was a Muslim trading colony in Athens.

Catholic westerners made up a sizable minority in Constantinople. They were mostly merchants and started to arrive well before the Fourth Crusade. While they had more political and economic clout than the Jews or Muslims, they were far less popular. The "Latins" or "Franks," as they were called regardless of their nationality, were considered to be crude, uncivilized, and, worst of all, false Christians. This hatred periodically flared up into anti-Latin riots.

One unique group that first made its entrance into Europe via Byzantium was the Gypsies. Originally from somewhere in India, they first appear in Byzantine annals in the mid-eleventh century. The story goes that Constantine IX was much troubled by wild beasts that were killing the game in his imperial hunting park. He hired a people called the Adsincani, who were famous fortunetellers and magicians, to kill the beasts with charmed (probably poisoned) meat. The term "Adsincani" is the root word for Gypsy in many European languages, such as "Tsiganes" in French. Gypsies are mentioned in more detail in a twelfth-century account, in which they are said to have been bear keepers and soothsayers, two occupations still practiced by some Gypsies in the Balkans:

> "They place dyed thread on the head and on the entire body of the animal. Then they would cut these threads and offer them along with parts of the animal's hair as amulets, and as a cure from diseases and the evil eye. Others, who are called Athinganoi, [another Byzantine term for Gypsies] would have snakes wound around them, and they would tell one person that he was born under an evil star, and the other under a lucky star; and they would also prophesy about forthcoming good and ill fortunes."[5]

Another outsider group was the slaves. Slaves were not of any single ethnicity, but so many of them were taken from the Slavic lands that our word "slave" comes from the word "Slav." Dalmatia became a slave coast, where Slavs were shipped to Constantinople or to western lands for sale. Other ethnic groups were taken as well, and in medieval warfare the victorious side commonly enslaved some of the defeated population. While slaves were numerous, the Byzantine

---

5. Soulis, "The Gypsies in the Byzantine Empire," pp. 146–47. Used by permission.

economy should not be seen as a slave economy. It did not rely on slaves to the same extent as the antebellum South or the colonial West Indies. Slaves had few rights, but in the cruel and unpredictable world of the Middle Ages, they often had more security than the free poor.

The Military

Byzantium was constantly at war, but it was not an especially bellicose culture. Most of its military strategy was based on defense. When their large armies and strong system of border forts did not dissuade invaders, emperors generally preferred to negotiate with the enemy or buy them off. But when all else failed, the Byzantines proved to be deadly foes.

The army was divided into two main components—infantry and cavalry. The old Roman army depended on heavily armored infantry fighting in close formation. This standard had to change when the empire faced nomads who fought with bows on horseback. Both the Romans and their rivals, the Persians, learned from these nomads and incorporated mounted archers into their fighting forces. Byzantine cavalry would soon become the pride of the army. Horsemen enjoyed more prestige and pay than the infantry.

Cavalry would ride into battle covered with metal armor. This armor was called chain mail, a flexible but tough suit made of interlocking metal rings. They would also wear metal plates called greaves to protect the legs, and a metal helmet. The entire suit weighed up to forty pounds. Shields provided additional protection. The standard weapons were the bow, sword, and long spear. Each unit would have a distinctive color and uniform so they could be told apart in battle, an innovation that was not used in the west until the sixteenth century.

Although cavalry were highly trained and effective, they were expensive to equip and maintain. The bulk of the army continued to be infantry. They favored lighter armor, but shields and helmets were always used. Spears and swords were popular, as were heavy axes for the Varangian Guard.

Knights and common soldier in the First Crusade

Nineteenth-century rendering of Crusaders, showing a common soldier and two knights. Their armor is chain mail, made by joining thousands of metal links. This type of armor was common both in Byzantium and the West. The more familiar plate armor seen in movies and drawings didn't develop until the late fourteenth and early fifteenth centuries.

SOURCE: *Historic Costume in Pictures*, by Braun & Schneider (Dover Publications, Inc., 1975).

Scouts would range ahead of an advancing army and report back on terrain and enemy movements. Engineers would build bridges and siege equipment, while camp followers provided drink and comfort for the soldiers.

Unlike in western kingdoms, where armies were called up for a season or two from among feudal lords, the Byzantines had a large standing army. These professionals were paid depending on rank, and as in other parts of Byzantine society, there was good opportunity for advancement.

Partly to reduce the large cost of such an army, and partly to have a regular force on the borders, the Byzantines developed the theme system. Soldiers were paid in land. This arrangement kept them in the border area they were supposed to protect and gave them a vested interest in fighting.

The Byzantines made a detailed study of war, and many strategy manuals survive. Tricks would be used to dishearten the enemy— such as ambushes, sending incriminating letters to enemy officers, and encouraging the enemy to come out onto an open plain where the Byzantine cavalry could be used to its full advantage. In the case of an invasion, the defenders of a theme would immediately warn their neighbors by lighting bonfires atop high hills. Cavalry would harass the enemy, and the infantry would set up ambushes in narrow defiles. In an open battle, the archers would rain arrows down on the enemy as the infantry advanced in close order shouting, "The Cross has Conquered!"[6]

Byzantine tactics varied with the people they faced. The Turks were the most feared enemy, but the Byzantine cavalry was generally stronger and preferred to fight them in open battle. The Arabs were also a serious risk, but they didn't fight well in cold or rainy weather. The Byzantines found the Latins to be overconfident and easy to lure into traps. The Slavs and Bulgars liked to set ambushes themselves, but in a fair fight they were generally no match for Byzantine discipline.

---

6. Schreiner, p. 80. Used by permission of the University of Chicago Press. © 1997 the University of Chicago.

The navy was never as prestigious or effective as the army. Its main strength was Greek fire, a primitive form of napalm that could be cast in ceramic grenades or squirted out of bellows. The recipe was a highly guarded secret. Greek fire burned so fiercely that even water couldn't put it out. Its effect on the wooden ships of the day can be imagined. It was only superceded by the development of accurate artillery in the fourteenth century.

Ships were also equipped with rams to punch holes in enemy hulls. If the Byzantines enjoyed superior numbers, they would often come in close and fight it out with bows and hand weapons as if they were on land.

Naval battles were generally avoided, and ships were mostly used for patrols, blockades, pirate hunts, and the transportation of troops. Ships were of varying size and used both sails and oars, depending on the weather. Ships with up to three hundred men were used in battle. There are no precise figures for the Byzantine navy, but in its glory days the empire could assemble fleets of several hundred vessels of varying sizes.

The combined military numbered more than 350,000 men at its height, but by the time of the Palaiologoi it was less than ten thousand.

X.

A Gazetteer of Byzantine Monuments

───◈◈───

A complete list of all Byzantine monuments would fill this book. What follows are some of the more important and better-preserved buildings from the Byzantine era. All of the monuments listed are open to the public, but some of the churches and monasteries are still in use, so visiting hours may be limited. As conditions often change, contact the tourism board of the individual country before planning a visit.

There are many museums that boast interesting Byzantine collections. They are too numerous to list here, so this chapter is limited to those specifically dedicated to artifacts from the Byzantine period. Large national museums are also worth visiting, and one should not overlook the many delightful little museums that can be found in even the smallest towns of Greece, Turkey, and Italy.

Greece

Athens:

Athens' Byzantine Museum is the largest of its kind in the country and houses several reconstructions of early churches and an excellent collection of icons and frescos.

Corfu:

This city in westernmost Greece has an interesting Museum of Byzantine and Post-Byzantine Art that gives the visitor a good idea of how the Byzantine style affected later artists.

Dhafní:

The Monastery of Dhafní was built over an older sanctuary of Apollo in the fifth or sixth century. Despite its high walls, it was sacked by the Crusaders in 1205. The church dates to the eleventh century and contains some fine mosaics. The central dome shows Christ Pantokrator ("Ruler of All") surrounded by Biblical figures. There is a wine festival here in September and October.

Dhidhimótikho:

This town on the northeastern coast has the remains of a Byzantine port, including imposing fortifications of the thirteenth century. They are very well-preserved and give a good idea of what the enemies of Byzantium had to face.

Island of Lesvos:

This Aegean island has a Byzantine Museum with an interesting collection of icons in the island's capital, Mitilíni.

Island of Patmos:

This island, where St. John the Divine had the vision that makes up the Book of Revelation, was an important Byzantine holy center. There is a Monastery of St. John on the island. In the chapel of Theotokos are twelfth-century frescoes of the Trinity and other religious figures. The archangels Michael and Gabriel are dressed as Byzantine emperors. The library displays medieval illustrated manuscripts.

Dome mosaic showing the baptism of Christ at the Monastery of Dhafní, Greece. The monastery was founded in the fifth or sixth century on the site of a sanctuary to the pagan god Apollo. The mosaics date to the eleventh century.
SOURCE: Laura Hollengreen.

Dome mosaic showing the Nativity at the Monastery of Dhafní, Greece.
SOURCE: Laura Hollengreen.

Gospels of Luke and John, St. John, Constantinople(?), twelfth century.

SOURCE: Dumbarton Oaks, Byzantine Photograph and Fieldwork Archives, Washington, DC.

Island of Sámos:

This island off the coast of Asia Minor has a Byzantine and Ecclesiastical Museum with icons from the island's monasteries.

Kastoriá:

This city in western Greece, near the Albanian border, has a Byzantine Museum.

Mistra:

One of the last holdouts of Byzantium, this medieval town is well preserved. The buildings are mostly from the fourteenth and fifteenth century. A stroll through the narrow streets, with houses and churches on every side, will make visitors feel as if they have stepped back to the last days of the empire. A visit that does justice to this site takes a full day, and the Palace of the Despots, one of the few surviving Byzantine government buildings in all of Greece, should not be missed.

Mount Athos:

This monastery complex has been an Orthodox refuge and pilgrimage center since the tenth century. Its location on a steep hill at the end of a long, rocky promontory has not always saved it from invaders. The monks, following an old tradition, are divided into those who live communally, and those who live on their own, worshiping according to a more individualistic rule. There are twenty monasteries here, including Russian, Bulgarian, and Serb communities. The many churches house icons and other examples of Orthodox Church art, including a striking dome mosaic of Christ Pantokrator holding the Bible under one arm. While the art and views of the sea are splendid, the fact that Mt. Athos is a functioning

Fourteenth-century murals at the Vatopedhi Church on Mt. Athos. A massive and wealthy monastery, Mt. Athos was second only to Constantinople as the spiritual center of the Orthodox Church and still has great importance today.
SOURCE: School of Architecture, College of Architecture, Planning, and Landscape Architecture, University of Arizona.

monastery complex in the traditional Orthodox style is what makes it so worth a visit. Only men are allowed inside and a permit is required in advance.

Néa Ankhíalos:

Near Vólos, north of Athens, is an important excavation of an early Byzantine town. Nine basilicas and several other remains have been found here, all dating from the fourth to the sixth centuries. While it is not as impressive as the complete buildings that are scattered across the Greek countryside, this site will be a worthwhile stop for those interested in archaeology.

208

Osios Loukás (or Hosios Loukás):

Between Athens and Delphi is the extensive Monastery of St. Luke Stíris. Its location atop a high hill provides wonderful views of the surrounding countryside. The monastery is dedicated to a local tenth-century hermit. The hermit predicted that Crete would be liberated by a man named Romanos. Romanos II fulfilled the prophecy and built the larger of the two churches here in 961 in his honor. There's also an eleventh-century church with brickwork imitating Arabic script. The monastery contains a museum of Byzantine sculpture, excellent mosaics from the life of Jesus, and crypts decorated with frescoes.

Rendína:

This small village seventy-one kilometers outside Thessaloniki has the ruins of a Byzantine fort. The ruins are in good condition.

Thessaloniki:

This city was the gateway from the Mediterranean into the Balkans and was an important center of trade long before Byzantine times. For much of Byzantine history, Thessaloniki was the empire's second city. During the Latin occupation it became the capital of a Crusader kingdom. Its recapture in 1246 by the empire of Nicaea was seen as a major moral and military victory.

There are several important Byzantine and early Christian buildings here. Panayía Akheiropoíetos, completed about 470, is one of the earliest churches still in use. It is similar in design to the basilicas in Syria.

The Ayios Yeóryios dates from the late third century and has mosaics from the late fourth century. It still has a minaret from the Turkish period, when it was used a mosque.

The Ayía Sophía dates from the eighth century, or perhaps even earlier, and has the best mosaics in the city.

The Arch of Galerius commemorates the co-emperor's victory over the Persians in 297. Only one section remains, bearing a relief of a triumphal parade and other military themes. The city also has other churches and a Byzantine Museum.

Zákynthos:

This town is on an island of the same name, one of the Ionian chain off the west coast of Greece. The town has a Museum of Byzantine Art.

Israel

Bethlehem:

The Basilica of the Nativity is built over the traditional site of the manger, the birthplace of Jesus. Constantine founded a church here, but it burned down and was rebuilt by Justinian in 531. There are several good mosaics. It is said that when the Persians invaded the region in the seventh century they burned all the churches but this one because the mosaic of the Three Wise Men shows them wearing Persian garb. Parts of the floor mosaics of the original church of Constantine still survive.

Jerusalem:

This city was the main pilgrimage site in Byzantine territory. The most important of its many churches is the Church of the Holy Sepulchre. It was built by Constantine over the purported site of Christ's crucifixion and burial, and finished in the year 335. Constantine's mother Helena (now St. Helena) is said to have found the True Cross here. The church was rebuilt and enlarged several times, and most of the present-day structure dates from the Crusader period. The tomb and the site of the Crucifixion are both inside the church. The church is currently divided among six religious groups: Greek Orthodox, Armenian Orthodox, Franciscan, Syrian, Coptic, and Ethiopian.

The Serbian monastery of Ravanica in central Serbia was founded by Prince
Lazar Hrebeljanovic (1371–1389) and his family. In 1375, Lazar was able to get
the Byzantines to recognize the legality of the Serbian patriarchate, ending almost
30 years of schism. He was killed fighting the Ottomans in the Battle of Kosovo,
also known as the Field of Blackbirds, and proclaimed a saint shortly thereafter.
His feast day is still celebrated by the Serbs. Lazar retained close ties with Byzantium throughout his reign, as is evidenced by the Byzantine style of this building.
SOURCE: Laura Hollengreen.

Because of this diversity, there is a wide variety of church art here from around the world, and the visitor can make some interesting comparisons.

Italy

Cefalu:

This small Sicilian town has one of the most beautiful Byzantine-era churches in Italy. Built by the Normans in the twelfth century, it is decorated inside with Byzantine columns, Gothic arches, and wonderfully preserved mosaics. The large figure of Christ is most striking. This church and San Vitale in Ravenna are arguably the best examples of Byzantine-style mosaics in Italy.

Florence:

At the southwestern edge of the historic city stands San Miniato al Monte, an eleventh-century church with a thirteenth-century Byzantine-style mosaic of Christ between the Virgin and the martyred warrior St. Minias.

Murano:

This suburb of Venice is the home of the Santa Maria e Donato, a seventh-century basilica rebuilt in the ninth and twelfth centuries. It has beautiful Byzantine columns and a twelfth-century floor mosaic.

Padua:

The church of Santa Sofia is a good example of ninth- or tenth-century Byzantine architecture, featuring a large apse with several spacious niches. The town also has several other early churches with Byzantine influences.

Piazza Armerina:

A few miles southwest of this little town is the Villa Imperiale, the mansion of Maximian. It now lies in ruins, but the well-preserved floor mosaics make this worth a visit. The lack of walls makes it easy to see the floor plan and get a good idea of the layout of a fourth-century palace. The palace included baths, an aqueduct, private apartments, and a large atrium.

Ravenna:

As the Byzantine capital in Italy, Ravenna has churches and mosaics that rival those of Constantinople.

The sixth-century church of San Vitale has exquisite mosaics in an unusual octagonal floor plan. One famous mosaic shows Justinian and his entourage, including the general Belisarius. Next to it is another mosaic with Theodora and her assistants.

Just next to the church is the fifth-century Mausoleum of Galla Placidia, the sister of the western emperor Honorius, with equally good mosaics in a lively classical style. One shows stags drinking from the Holy Fount. The roof shows a cross in a starry sky.

Also in Ravenna is the Baptistry of the Orthodox, originally an old Roman bathhouse with many mosaics, including one of the baptism of Jesus.

Nearby is the Archbishop's Palace, which has many Byzantine artifacts including the elaborate ivory throne of Maximian.

The church of San Apollinare Nuovo, built in the sixth century, has extensive mosaics showing the life and Passion of Jesus.

San Giovanni Evangelista contains mosaics showing scenes from the Fourth Crusade.

The expressive but unfinished Mausoleum of Theodoric is also worth a visit for its unusual, tower-like appearance. Inside is a porphyry tub that supposedly once held Theodoric's remains.

Near Ravenna, San Apollinare in Classe has mosaics and inscriptions from the sixth century.

Baptistery ceiling at San Vitale, Ravenna. This brilliant dome mosaic dates to the sixth century and shows John baptizing Christ, surrounded by images of the apostles.

SOURCE: School of Architecture, College of Architecture, Planning, and Landscape Architecture, University of Arizona.

Column capital from San Vitale, Ravenna. This capital displays the elaborate style typical of the later Byzantine period.

SOURCE: School of Architecture, College of Architecture, Planning, and Landscape Architecture, University of Arizona.

Rome:

While the Roman monuments are not as impressive as the ones in Ravenna, Rome has a great number of Byzantine sites. So many monuments in the city date from the early Christian era that only an illustrative sample can be given here.

Santa Sabina is a basilica of the fifth century with interesting examples of early church architecture and decoration, including mosaics.

The Column of Phokas, dating to 608, was the last monument to be erected in the old Roman Forum.

The nearby Santa Maria Antiqua is an eighth-century church with many fine frescoes.

Also in the Forum is the imposing Basilica of Constantine. It was begun in 306 by Maxentius and finished by Constantine, although the date of its completion remains uncertain. While mostly destroyed by an earthquake in 847, what remains gives a good idea of the layout and impressive size of the original structure.

Another relic of the founder of Byzantium is the Arch of Constantine, erected in 315 to commemorate his victory over Maxentius. It is covered with interesting reliefs, most taken from earlier monuments.

The Santa Agnese fuori le Mura was built by Constantia, Constantine's daughter, in 342. It was built atop some well-preserved catacombs that once housed the bones of St. Agnes. A seventh-century mosaic in the church shows the saint, who was famed for her chastity.

Constantia and her sister Helena have a mausoleum that is now the church of Santa Costanza. The fourth-century mosaics are perhaps the oldest known examples with Christian themes.

There are several sets of catacombs beneath Rome. These were burying grounds for the early Christians and have many well-preserved early chapels.

Some of the best mosaics in Rome are to be found at the sixth-century Sts. Cosmas and Damian, including the Lamb of God on a mount from which the four rivers of the Gospels flow.

Torcello:

This town near Venice has a seventh-century cathedral, L'Assunta, altered in the ninth and eleventh centuries. Decoration includes a fine mosaic of the Last Judgment. There is also some excellent late Byzantine grillwork of carved stone.

Venice:

San Marco is the most famous monument in Venice and is one of the best examples of Byzantine-style church buildings in Italy. The five-domed church is in the shape of a Greek cross. The floor plan may have been based on the Church of the Apostles in Constantinople, now lost. The original church on this site was built in the early ninth century and contained the body of St. Mark the Evangelist. The church burned down during a riot in 976 and the present building dates to the mid- to late eleventh century. The interior has excellent eleventh-century Byzantine-style mosaics, much restored in later centuries. One of the best depicts Christ between the Virgin and Saint Mark. The central bronze door at the entrance is decorated in relief and is of Byzantine manufacture. Another door, of silver, is called the Porta di San Clemente and is said to have been a gift from Alexios Komnenos. In the church treasury is an impressive collection of loot from the Fourth Crusade, including several reliquaries and four copper horses that used to stand in the Hippodrome. In the Chapel of the Crucifix are six marble columns with gilded Byzantine capitals.

Jordan

Jerash:

This extensive set of ruins is about fifty kilometers north of Amman. The town dates back to Neolithic times and became a city during the reign of Alexander the Great. While much of this site is pre-Byzantine, it gives a good idea of the layout of a Roman city. Archaeologists have uncovered more than a dozen Byzantine churches.

Madaba:

This town thirty kilometers south of Amman was a prosperous provincial center during the Byzantine era. The Church of St. George has a large sixth-century mosaic map of Palestine and lower Egypt. The Nile, the Dead Sea, and other geographic features are clearly shown. It also includes a map of Jerusalem showing the Church of the Holy Sepulchre. The Church of the Apostles has another large mosaic, this one showing all twelve apostles.

Mt. Nebo:

This small mountain range is a series of three peaks about ten kilometers west of Madaba. Atop one of them, called Siyagha, are the ruins of a fourth-century church, much expanded in later years. Some excellent mosaic floors have been uncovered here, including one of riders hunting African beasts.

Syria

Aleppo:

Near the city of Aleppo is the Qal'at Si'man, the Basilica of St. Simeon Stylites. This is the site where the famous ascetic spent more than forty years atop a tall column. It had already become a pilgrimage center during his life, and when he died in 459, this church was constructed. The church is now in ruins, but the floor plan can still be seen. The column itself is little more than a lump of stone. Pilgrims have been chipping away mementos since Simeon's death.

Qal'at Si'man, Syria, south facade of the south basilica. This church is on the site where St. Simeon Stylites spent most of his life sitting atop a pillar. The church was probably built by the emperor Zeno (474–91) shortly after the holy man's death.
SOURCE: Dumbarton Oaks, Byzantine Photograph and Fieldwork Archives, Washington, DC. Photograph by Richard Anderson.

Crac des Chevaliers:

While this castle is not strictly a Byzantine site, it is one of the most impressive and best-preserved Crusader strongholds. It stands on a low hill overlooking the pass between Turkey, Lebanon, and Syria. The castle, which owes much of its style to Byzantine fortress architecture, was never taken by storm.

Damascus:

The Ummayad Mosque, deep in the city's fascinating Old City, has a complex history. There was originally a Temple of Jupiter on the site, but it was converted into a church in the fourth century. The Muslims converted the eastern half of it into a mosque when they took the city in 636, but allowed the Christians to worship in the western half of the building. Little remains of these structures, because that building was leveled in the early eighth century to make way for the present mosque, one of the finest in the Levant. The caliph at the time wanted it to have the most beautiful decoration available, and that meant hiring Byzantines to cover it with mosaics. Many of these still exist, including those on the city Treasury, a small tower located in the mosque's main courtyard. The Byzantines followed the strictures of Islam by showing no human figures; all the mosaics are of plants and abstract designs.

Turkey

Cappadocia:

This region in central Turkey was once very volcanic. The eruptions left a thick layer of soft tufa stone. Erosion and the wind have carved this stone into fantastic shapes, and people from all periods of history have carved houses, churches, and even entire cities under the surface. Some of the houses are still lived in today. There are many churches that can be visited, and several have simple painted interiors in a distinctive local style.

Istanbul (formerly Constantinople):

The capital of Byzantium has suffered from the Fourth Crusade and extensive Ottoman rebuilding, but it is still the best place to see Byzantine art and architecture. While most of the buildings are from the Turkish era, the main streets still follow the old Byzantine plan,

These unique rock-cut dwellings in Cappadocia, in central Asia Minor, were carved from soft volcanic tufa. The earliest date to prehistoric times. During the Byzantine period, many monks lived in shelters such as these and carved churches out of the stone.

SOURCE: Turkish Tourist Office.

so a stroll through the city gives the visitor a good feel for what it was like in Byzantine times.

The main attraction, of course, is the Hagia Sophia (now called the Aya Sophia). It was the site of some of the most important moments in Byzantine history, including the ceremony to proclaim new emperors. The building dates from the time of Justinian and includes large sections of mosaics. They were plastered over when the church was converted into a mosque, and so they have been very well preserved. The building is now a museum and the mosaics have been uncovered. They show various emperors and empresses, and there are good descriptions of the images for sale at the site. The tour is also worthwhile, but leave some time to walk around on your own.

The Ottomans built the Blue Mosque partly on the old Hippodrome and partly where the imperial palace once stood. All that is left are some interesting fifth-century mosaics from one of the rooms. The mosaics are housed in a mosaic museum on site.

Rendering of a column capital from the Hagia Sophia by Cary Dosenbrock (1983). Earlier classic forms of column capitals gave way in the Byzantine period to more elaborate examples such as this.

SOURCE: School of Architecture, College of Architecture, Planning, and Landscape Architecture, University of Arizona.

The Hagia Eirene (now called the Aya Irini Kilisesi) was an important fourth-century church that was the site for the second ecumenical council. There is a giant mosaic cross on a gold background on the dome in the apse.

The Theodosian walls, dating to the fifth century, were built during the reign of Theodosius II. They protected the capital from numerous assaults and still stand to their full height in most places. A visit to the landward walls will show why so many of Byzantine's enemies failed to scale them.

Iznik (*Nicaea*):

One of the largest cities in the empire, Nicaea was the site of the first and seventh ecumenical councils. There are numerous Byzantine buildings here from various centuries, as well as a third-century wall, extensively rebuilt in the thirteenth century, which surrounds the city.

Lake Van:

This lake in eastern Turkey near the border with Iran has many fine churches on its eastern and southern shore. One especially interesting example is the Church of the Holy Cross, built in an Armenian style greatly influenced by Byzantine architecture. It has a high, pointed dome and a great number of fascinating stone reliefs.

Mardin:

Near the border with Syria is the town of Mardin, built on a steep slope. A short distance away is the Deir-Al-Zafaran, "the Saffron Monastery." It is on a high hill for defensive purposes. It has two early churches. In the cliffs nearby are caves where monks used to live. East of Mardin is Mor Gabriel (the Qartmin Monastery). The seventh-century Church of Gabriel has several grand domes, some with decoration.

Trabzon (*Trebizond*):

Trebizond, on the southern shore of the Black Sea, became its own separate state during the Latin occupation of Constantinople. It remained independent throughout the Palaiologan era and was the last holdout of Byzantine power, lasting eight years longer than Constantinople. There are many Byzantine monuments in and around the city. About fifty kilometers south of the city is the Sumela Monastery. It takes a tough half hour to climb to the top of the steep hill, where the monastery looks out over a deep gorge of white water. The main church has several beautiful paintings from the fifteenth century showing some of the Komnenos dynasty.

Zeugma:

This town near the Syrian border has the excellent Byzantine castle of Gavur Kalesi (or Rum Kalesi, "Castle of the Greeks"). Of uncertain date, it sits atop a steep hill overlooking the Euphrates River. Despite being of immense strategic importance, the Turks were not able to take it until the thirteenth century. Locals say that St. John the Evangelist was buried here.

TIMELINE

—⟫•⟪—

286   Diocletian establishes divided rule

293   Diocletian establishes tetrarchy

312   Battle of Milvian Bridge

313   Edict of Milan recognizes Christianity as fully legal religion

324   Constantine establishes united rule

325   First ecumenical council at Nicaea, also called the first Council at Nicaea

330   Dedication of Constantinople at Byzantium

361   Julian attempts to reestablish paganism

381   Second ecumenical council at Constantinople, also called the first Council of Constantinople

395   Emperor Theodosius, last man to rule over unified Roman Empire, dies

410	Visigoths sack Rome
413	Theodosian land walls completed at Constantinople
431	Third ecumenical council at Ephesus, alternately the councils of Ephesus or the Council of Ephesus
451	Fourth ecumenical council at Chalcedon, also called the Council of Chalcedon
476	Western Emperor Romulus Augustulus, last emperor of the West, overthrown
537	Justinian completes Hagia Sophia
553	Fifth ecumenical council at Constantinople, also called the second Council of Constantinople or one-half of the Quinisext Council
630	Final victory over Persia
632	Death of Muhammad
633	Arabs expand out of Arabia
680–81	Sixth ecumenical council at Constantinople, also called the third Council of Constantinople or one-half of the Quinisext Council
681	First Bulgarian empire founded
718	Arabs fail to take Constantinople
726	Leo III introduces iconoclasm
730	Iconoclasm proclaimed as official policy

750	Caliphate moves from Damascus to Baghdad
787	Seventh ecumenical council at Nicaea, also called the second Council of Nicaea
800	Charlemagne crowned emperor of the Romans
843	Iconoclasm abolished
863	Cyril and Methodius go on mission to the Slavs
988	Vladimir, prince of Kiev, baptized
1071	Battle of Manzikert
1096–99	First Crusade
1145	Papal Crusade bull issued
1147–49	Second Crusade
1186	Second Bulgarian empire founded
1187	Muslims retake Jerusalem
1189–92	Third Crusade
1202–4	Fourth Crusade
1204–61	Latin Empire of Constantinople
1261	Byzantine reconquest of Constantinople
1274	The second Council of Lyons, Churches united
1347–50	Black Death sweeps through Mediterranean and Europe

1366	Emperor John V Palaiologos journeys to western provinces
1396	Hungarian campaign against the Turks
1399	Emperor Manuel II journeys to west to seek aid against the Ottomans
1438–45	Council of Ferrara-Florence, Churches united by signed decree in 1439
1453	Ottomans capture Constantinople
1456	Ottomans conquer Athens
1460	Ottomans conquer Mistra
1461	Ottomans conquer Trebizond

LIST OF BYZANTINE EMPERORS

⟦────⟧

Below is a list of the emperors and co-emperors from Diocletian to the fall of Constantinople. There were dozens of pretenders to the title throughout this period, especially in the fourth and fifth centuries. They are not named unless they controlled substantial territory and are mentioned in the text. The names are given the Latin spelling until the dynasty of Herakleios, by which time Byzantium was, in essence, only an eastern empire. While the exile dynasties of Epiros and Trebizond are not listed, the names of the Nicaean rulers are given since theirs was the empire that retook Constantinople from the Crusaders.

The United Roman Empire and the Tetrarchy

Dates	Name
284–305	Diocletian, Augustus of the East
286–305	Maximian, Augustus of the West
305–10	Galerius, Augustus of the East
305–6	Constantius I, Augustus of the West

306–7	Severus II, Augustus of the West
308–24	Licinius, Augustus of various regions depending on political circumstance
306–24	Constantine I, proclaimed Augustus of the West in 306 but not recognized until 313
306–12	Maxentius, Augustus in Italy
310–13	Maximinus Daia, Augustus of the East
324–37	Constantine I, emperor of unified Rome
337–40	Constantine II, Augustus of Britain, Gaul and Spain
337–50	Constans, Augustus of Italy, Africa, Illyricum, Macedonia, and Achaea. Took Britain, Gaul and Spain after 340
337–61	Constantius II, Augustus of most of the East. Emperor of unified Rome after 350
361–63	Julian, emperor of unified Rome
363–64	Jovian, emperor of unified Rome
364–75	Valentinian I, Augustus of the West
364–78	Valens, Augustus of the East
367–83	Gratian, co-Augustus of the West, first with Valentinian I, then with Valentinian II
383–88	Maximus, co-Augustus of the West with Valentinian II

375–92	Valentinian II, co-Augustus of the West, first with Gratian, then with Maximus
379–95	Theodosius I, Augustus of the East, from 392 was the last emperor of unified Rome

The Empire of the West

395	**PARTITION – WESTERN EMPIRE**
395–423	Honorius
423–25	Johannes
425–55	Valentinian III
455	Petronius Maximus
455–56	Avitus
457–61	Majorian
461–65	Libius Severus III
467–72	Anthemius
472	Olybrius
473–74	Glycerius
474–75	Julius Nepos
475–76	Romulus Augustulus

The Empire of the East

395   PARTITION – EASTERN EMPIRE

Dynasty of Theodosius

395–408   Arcadius

408–450   Theodosius II

450–57   Marcian

Dynasty of Leo

457–74   Leo I

474   Leo II

474–91   Zeno

491–518   Anastasius I

Dynasty of Justinian

518–27   Justin I

527–65   Justinian I

565–78   Justin II

578–82   Tiberius II

582–602   Maurice

602–10   Phokas

Dynasty of Herakleios

610–41   Herakleios

641   Constantine III

641   Heraclonas

641–68   Constans II

668–85   Constantine IV

685–95   Justinian II

695–98   Leontios

698–705   Tiberius Apsimar

705–11   Justinian II (restored)

Mixed Dynasty

711–13   Philippikos Vardanes

713–15   Anastasios II

715–17   Theodosios III

Isaurian Dynasty

717–41   Leo III

741–75   Constantine V

775–80   Leo IV

780–97   Constantine VI

797–802   Irene

802–11   Nikephoros I

811   Stavrakios

811–13   Michael I

813–20   Leo V

Phrygian Dynasty

820–29   Michael II

829–42   Theophilos

842–67   Michael III

Macedonian Dynasty

867–86   Basil I

886–912   Leo VI

912–13   Alexander

913–59   Constantine VII

920–44   Romanos I

959–63   Romanos II

963–69   Nikephoros II Phokas

969–76   John I Tzimiskes

976–1025   Basil II

1025–28   Constantine VIII

1028–50   Empress Zoe

1028–34   Romanos III Argyros

1034–41   Michael IV

1041–42   Michael V Kalaphates

1042   Empresses Zoe and Theodora

1042–55   Constantine IX

1055–56   Empress Theodora

1056–57   Michael VI

Mixed Dynasties

1057–59   Isaac I Komnenos

1059–67   Constantine X Doukas

1067   Empress Eudokia

1068–71   Romanos IV Diogenes

1071–78   Michael VII Doukas

1078–81   Nikephoros III Botaneiates

Dynasty of the Komneni

1081–1118   Alexios I Komnenos

1118–43   John II Komnenos

1143–80   Manuel I Komnenos

1180–83   Alexios II Komnenos

1183–85   Andronikos I Komnenos

Dynasty of the Angeli

1185–95   Isaac II Angelos

1195–1203   Alexios III Angelos

1203–4   Isaac II (restored) with Alexios IV

1204   Alexios V Doukas Mourtzouphlos

1204   Loss of Constantinople

Laskarid Dynasty in Nicaea

1204–22	Theodore I Laskaris
1222–54	John III Doukas Vatatzes
1254–58	Theodore II Laskaris
1258–61	John IV Laskaris, co-emperor with Michael VIII Palaiologos from 1258

Dynasty of the Palaiologoi

1261–82	Michael VIII Palaiologos
1261	**RECAPTURE OF CONSTANTINOPLE**
1282–1328	Andronikos II Palaiologos
1328–41	Andronikos III Palaiologos
1341–76	John V Palaiologos
1347–54	John VI Cantacuzene
1376–79	Andronikos IV Palaiologos
1379–91	John V Palaiologos (restored)
1390	John VII Palaiologos
1391–1425	Manuel II Palaiologos
1425–48	John VIII Palaiologos

1449–53   Constantine XI Palaiologos

1453   **CAPTURE OF CONSTANTINOPLE BY**
May 29   **MEHMED II**

BIBLIOGRAPHY

Athanassiadi-Fowden, Polymnia. *Julian and Hellenism: An Intellectual Biography.* Oxford: Clarendon Press, 1981.

Benedict. *The Rule of St. Benedict.* Translated by Anthony Meisel and M.L. del Mastro. New York: Image Books, 1975.

Brown, Peter. *The World of Late Antiquity.* London: Thames & Hudson, Ltd., 1971, latest edition © 1987.

Brown, Robin. *Blue Guide: Greece.* 6th ed. New York: W.W. Norton, 1995.

Cameron, Averil. *The Mediterranean World in Late Antiquity, A.D. 395–600.* New York: Routledge, 1993.

Cavallo, Guglielmo, ed. *The Byzantines.* Translated by Thomas Dunlap, Teresa Lavender Fagan, and Charles Lambert. Chicago: The University of Chicago Press, 1997.

Cyril of Scythopolis. *Cyril of Scythopolis: The Lives of the Monks of Palestine.* Translated by R.M. Price. Kalamazoo, MI: Cistercian Publications, Inc., 1991.

Eusebius. *History of the Church.* Translated by G. A. Williamson. Revised by A. Louth. New York: Penguin Books, 1989.

———. *Life of Constantine.* Translated by Averil Cameron and Stuart G. Hall. Oxford: Clarendon Press, 1999.

Fraser, Angus. *The Gypsies.* Cambridge: Blackwell Publishers, Inc., 1995.

Gabrieli, Francesco. *Muhammad and the Conquests of Islam*. New York: McGraw-Hill, 1968.

Gibbon, Edward. *The Decline and Fall of the Roman Empire*. Edited by J.B. Bury. New York: F. DeFau & Company, 1906–7.

Guillou, André. "Functionaries." In *The Byzantines*. Edited by Guglielmo Cavallo, pp. 197–229. Chicago: University of Chicago Press, 1997. *See also* Cavallo.

Halperin, Ch. J. "Bulgars and Slavs in the First Bulgarian Empire: A Reconsideration of the Historiography." In *Archivum Eurasiae Medii Aevi* III, pp. 183–200. Lisse, Netherlands: Peter de Ridder Press, 1983.

Harris, Jonathan, "Byzantines in Renaissance Italy." In *ORB: The Online Reference Book for Medieval Studies*, ed. K. Talarico. New York: College of Staten Island, CUNY, 2002. http://www.the-orb.net (accessed May 27, 2004).

Head, Constance. *Imperial Byzantine Portraits*. New Rochelle, NY: Caratzas Publishing Company, Inc., 1982.

Herbermann, Charles, Andrew MacEarlean, Edward Pace, Condé Pallen, Thomas Shahan, and John Wynne. *The Catholic Encyclopedia: An International Work of Reference on the Constitution, Doctrine, Discipline, and History of the Catholic Church*. New York: Appleton, 1907–12.

Jeffreys, Elizabeth, editor. *Digenis Akritis: the Grottaferrata and Escorial Versions*. New York: Cambridge University Press, 1998.

Jones, J.R. Melville, trans. *The Siege of Constantinople 1453: Seven Contemporary Accounts*. Amsterdam: Adolf M. Hakkert-Publisher, 1972.

Jordan, Robert. "John of Phoberou: A Voice Crying in the Wilderness." In *Strangers to Themselves: The Byzantine Outsider*, edited by Dion Smythe, pp. 61–73. Burlington, VT: Ashgate Publishing Company, 2000.

Kazhdan, Alexander. "The Peasantry." In *The Byzantines*, edited by Guglielmo Cavallo, pp. 43–73. Chicago: University of Chicago Press, 1997. *See also* Cavallo.

MacMullen, Ramsay. *Paganism in the Roman Empire*. New Haven, CT: Yale University Press, 1981.

Mamertinus, Claudius. "A Speech of Thanks Given to the Emperor Julian." In *The Emperor Julian: Panegyric and Polemic*, edited by Samuel N.C. Lieu, pp. 3–38. Liverpool, UK: Liverpool University Press, 1989.

Mango, Cyril. "Saints." In *The Byzantines*, edited by Guglielmo Cavallo, pp. 255–80. Chicago: University of Chicago Press, 1997. *See also* Cavallo.

Marcellinus, Ammianus. *The Later Roman Empire*. Translated by Walter Hamilton. New York: Penguin Books, 1986.

McCormick, Michael. "Emperors." In *The Byzantines*, edited by Guglielmo Cavallo, pp. 230–54. Chicago: University of Chicago Press, 1997. *See also* Cavallo.

McDonagh, Bernard. *Blue Guide: Turkey*. 3rd ed. New York: W.W. Norton, 2001.

Nicol, Donald. *Church and Society in the Last Centuries of Byzantium: The Birkbeck Lectures, 1977*. New York: Cambridge University Press, 1979.

————. *The End of the Byzantine Empire*. Foundations of Medieval History Series. London: Edward Arnold, Ltd., 1979.

————. *The Immortal Emperor: The Life and Legend of Constantine Palaiologos, Last Emperor of the Romans*. New York: Cambridge University Press, 1992.

Nicolle, David. *Medieval Warfare Source Book*. London: Arms and Armour Press, 1995.

Norwich, John Julius. *A Short History of Byzantium*. New York: Alfred A. Knopf, 1997.

Oikonomides, Nicolas. "Entrepreneurs." In *The Byzantines*, edited by Guglielmo Cavallo, pp. 144–71. Chicago: University of Chicago Press, 1997. *See also* Cavallo.

Patlagean, Evelyne. "The Poor." In *The Byzantines*, edited by Guglielmo Cavallo, pp. 15–42. Chicago: University of Chicago Press, 1997. *See also* Cavallo.

Procopius. *Secret History*. Translated by Richard Atwater. Ann Arbor, MI: University of Michigan Press, 1961.

Psellus, Michael. "Chronographia." In *Fourteen Byzantine Rulers: The Chronographia of Michael Psellus*, edited by E.R.A. Sewter. New York: Penguin Books, 1979.

Rice, Tamara Talbot. *Everyday Life in Byzantium.* New York: Dorset Press, 1967.

Rodley, Lyn. *Byzantine Art and Architecture: An Introduction.* New York: Cambridge University Press, 1993.

Rosser, John. *Historical Dictionary of Byzantium.* London: The Scarecrow Press, Inc., 2001.

Runciman, Steven. *Byzantine Civilization.* London: Edward Arnold & Co., 1948.

————. *The Fall of Constantinople 1453.* New York: Cambridge University Press, 1991.

————. *The Last Byzantine Renaissance: The Wiles Lectures Given at Queens University Belfast, 1968.* New York: Cambridge University Press, 1970.

Salaman, Clement, Dorine van Oyen, William D. Wharton, and Jean-Pierre Mahé. *The Way of Hermes.* London: Duckbacks, 1999.

Scarre, Chris. *Chronicle of the Roman Emperors: The Reign-by-Reign Record of the Rulers of Imperial Rome.* London: Thames & Hudson, Ltd., 1995.

Schreiner, Peter. "Soldiers." In *The Byzantines*, edited by Guglielmo Cavallo, pp. 74–94. Chicago: University of Chicago Press, 1997. *See also* Cavallo.

Soulis, G.C. "The Gypsies in the Byzantine Empire and the Balkans in the Late Middle Ages." In *Dumbarton Oaks Papers,* No. 15 (1961), pp. 142–65.

Talbot, Alice-Mary. "Women." In *The Byzantines*, edited by Guglielmo Cavallo, pp. 117–143. Chicago: University of Chicago Press, 1997. *See also* Cavallo.

Treadgold, Warren. *A Concise History of Byzantium.* New York: Palgrave, 2001.

Vasiliev, A.A. *History of the Byzantine Empire.* Madison, WI: University of Wisconsin Press, 1952.

Villehardouin, Geoffroy de. "Conquest of Constantinople." In *Chronicles of the Crusades*, edited by Margaret Shaw. New York: Penguin Books, 1984.

Zosimus. *Zosimus: Historia Nova.* Translated by James Buchanan and Harold Davies. San Antonio, TX: Trinity University Press, 1967.

ABOUT THE AUTHOR

SOURCE: Almudena Alonso-Herrero.

SEAN MCLACHLAN earned his master's degree in archaeology, specializing in the medieval period, at the University of Missouri-Columbia. He has helped supervise excavations in Israel, Cyprus, Bulgaria and the United States. Now a full-time writer, Sean has published hundreds of articles in newspapers, the Reuters Wire Service, and magazines such as *The World and I, Ancient Egypt Magazine,* and *Global Journalist.* Besides writing, his greatest passion is travel. He has spent several years on the road, visiting more than twenty-five countries and exploring everything from the snow-capped mountains of Peru to the ancient monuments of Iran. When not making research trips to the United States, he lives in Madrid with his wife and best friend, Almudena.

INDEX

Page numbers in *italics* indicate illustrations

Abbasid caliphate, 84, 85, 96, 106, 108
Acacius, 50
Age of Migrations, 1, 3–4
agriculture, 175–176
Alaric (Visigoth king), 41, 42
Albania, 152
Alemanni, 3
Aleppo, 101, 147, 217
Alexander, 93
Alexios Komnenos, 111, 112, 115–117
Alexios II, 122
Alexios III, 125, 127, 129
Alexios IV, 125, 126, 128
Alexios V Doukas, 128, 129
Ammianus Marcellinus, 37, 38
ampulla (pilgrim flask), *191*
amulet of St. Simeon Stylites, 35, *35*
Anadolu Hisar castle, 146
Anastasius, 50, 52–53
Andronikos Doukas, 108, 109
Andronikos Komnenos, 122–123
Andronikos II, 137, 138, 140, 141
Andronikos III, 141
Angeli, Dynasty of the, 236
Angles, 47
Anglo-Saxon England, 47

Anna (wife of Andronikos III), 141
Anna (wife of Vladimir of Kiev), 99
Anthony, Saint, 27
Antioch, 67, 117
aqueducts, 2, *2*
Arabia, 68
Arabs, 69–71, 77–78, *78*, 86, 94, 96, 101, 115
Arcadius, 40
Archbishop's Palace, 213
Arch of Constantine, 215
Arch of Galerius, 210
Arians, 39
Arius (Egyptian priest), 17, 18, 23
Armenia/Armenians, 24, 63, 64–65, 66, 108, 109
Asia Minor, 18, 108, 109, 115, 131, 140, 141, 175, 176, 209, *220*
Athenaïs Eudokia, 43
Athens, 203
Attila, 45
Augustus, title of, 12
Avars, 64, 67
Aya Sophia. *See* Hagia Sophia
Ayía Sophía, 209
Ayios Yeóryios, 209

245

Baghdad, 84, 85, 106, 108, 147
Balkans, 67
Baptistry of the Orthodox, 213
Basil, 88, 90
Basil II (Basil the Bulgar-Slayer),
    98–99, 101
Basilica of Bishop Euphrasius, 56, 56
Basilica of Constantine, 215
Basilica of St. Simeon Stylites, 217, 218
Battle of Catalaunian Fields, 5
Battle of Hastings, 111
Belisarius, 61–62, 63–64
Benedict, Saint, 27, 30, 33
Bethlehem, 210
Black Death, 142
Blue Mosque, 221
Blues, 52, 57–58, 73, 75
Bosnia, 103
Brankoviæ, Maria, 155–156
Bringas, 96
Britain, 47
bronze belt buckle, 76
bronze weight (5th-6th century), 185
bubonic plague, 63, 142
Bulgars/Bulgaria, 72, 75, 77, 78, 85,
    87, 88, 93–94, 96–97, 98–99,
    101, 103, 125, 143
Byzantine costumes/clothing. See also
    lifestyle
    imperial, 173
    military and Crusaders, 199, 199
    secular & religious, 191
Byzantine monuments
    in Greece, 203–204, 205, 207–210
    in Israel, 210, 211, 212
    in Italy, 212–213, 214, 215–216
    in Jordan, 216–217
    in Syria, 217–219
    in Turkey, 219, 220, 221–223

Caesar, title of, 12
Cameron, Averil, 47

Cantacuzene, John, 141
Cappadocia, 219, 220
Castle of the Greeks, 223
catacombs, 215
Cefalu, 212
chariot races, 20, 52, 57–58
Charlemagne, 84
Chosroes I (Persian king), 62–63
Chosroes II (Persian king), 68, 69
church councils
    Chalcedon, 45, 50
    Constantinople, first, 39, 222
    Constantinople, third, 72–73
    Ephesus, 45
    Florence, 150, 154
    Nicaea, first, 18
    Nicaea, second, 290
churches and cathedrals. See also
    monasteries
    Church of Gabriel, 222
    Church of the Holy Cross, 222
    Church of the Holy Sepulchre, 19,
        210, 211, 212
    Hagia Eirene (Aya Irini Kilisesi), 222
    Hagia Sophia, 58, 59, 60, 61, 61,
        69, 99, 135, 141–142, 162, 165,
        166, 221
    L'Assunta, 216
    Panagia ton Chalkeon, 110
    San Apollinare Nuovo, 213
    San Marco, 216
    Santa Agnese fuori le Mura, 215
    Santa Costanza, 215
    Santa Maria Antiqua, 215
    Santa Sofia, 212
    San Vitale, 213, 214
    St. George, 217
    St. Ripsime, 51, 51
    St. Simeon Stylites, 217, 218
    Vatopedhi Church, 208, 208
Church of the Holy Sepulchre, 19,
    210, 211, 212

civil war, 5
column capital from Hagia Sophia, 221
column capital from San Vitale, 214
Column of Phokas, 215
Communion of the Apostles, silver
    paten, 195, 195
Constans, 24
Constans II, 70
Constantine, 13, 14–18, 20, 23
Constantine II, 24–25
Constantine V, 81
Constantine VII, 93–94
Constantine VIII, 103–104
Constantine IX, 106
Constantine XI Palaiologos, 153–159,
    161–165
Constantinople
    Byzantium's transformation into,
        18, 20
    monuments in Istanbul, 219,
        221–222
    siege of, 156–159, 160, 161–165
Constantius, 12–13
Coptic tapestry, 80, 80
Corfu, 204
Cosmas, Saint, 215
councils, church. See church councils
Crac des Chevaliers, 218
Crete, 86, 94, 96
Crimea, 67
crops, 176
Crusades and Crusaders
    First, 112, 114, 115–118, 199, 199
    Second, 118
    Third, 123, 125
    Fourth, 125–129, 131–132
culture. See also lifestyle
    artisans and craftsmen, 186, 189
    and business, 186
    Byzantine influence on Renaissance,
        166, 170

Palaiologan Renaissance, 148
    trade and international influence,
        79, 81
    Western and Eastern differences,
        9–10
currency, 16, 16, 183–184, 184
Cyprus, 96
Cyrillic alphabet, 88
Cyril (monk and linguist), 87–88

Damascus, 219
Damian, Saint, 215
Decius, 4
Dhafní, 204, 205
Dhidhimótikho, 204
Digenis Akritis, 178
Diocletian, 1, 5–6, 9, 10, 11–12, 13
dynasties, 171–172, 229–238

earrings, gold (10th century), 188
economy
    under Alexios Komnenos, 116–117
    under Anastasius, 52
    under Andronikos II, 140
    under Basil II, 101
    businessmen and trade, 182–184,
        186, 189
    under Constantine VII, 94
    under Constantine XI, 156
    Eastern empire, 9
    history of, 182–184, 186, 189
    under Irene, 85
    under Isaac II Angelos, 123
    under Justinian, 54
    under Justin II, 64
    under Maurice, 66
    and religion, 9
    under Tiberius Constantine, 66
    Western empire, 9–10
ecumenical councils. See church
    councils

education
  legacy of Constantine IX, 106
  of Moravians in Orthodoxy, 87–88
  in the 3rd century, 9
  in the 15th century, 153
  Renaissance, 147–148
  under Theodosius II, 43
  trade between scholars, 196
  of women, 179
Egypt/Egyptians, 27, 45–46, 67, 70
emigration of Greeks, 147
emperors/empresses, Byzantine,
    171–172, 229–238. *See also
    specific names*
epidemics, 63, 112, 142
Epiros, 131
Eusebius, 14, 23, 24

farming, 175–178
Field of the Blackbirds (battle), 145
Florence, 212
food and diet, 176, 182–183
Franks/France, 3, 47, 83
fresco of Christ (14th century), *138*

Galata, 142, 158, 166
Galerius, 12–14
Gaul, 42, 45, 47
Gavur Kalesi, 223
Gennadios (monk), 154, 157, 165–166
Genoa, 134
Genoese, 158, 166
Germanic fibulae (clasps), 65, *65*
Germanic tribes, 2. *See also specific
    tribal names*
Germany, 125
Giustiniani Longo, Geovanni, 157,
    158–159, 164
Glagolitic alphabet, 87–88
Golden Horn, 18, 126
Gospel book leaf (11th-12th century),
    100, *100*

Goths, 3, 37
government decentralization, 11
Grand Company of Catalans, 140
Gratian, 36, 39
Greek fire, 71, 77, 98, 201
Greens, 52, 57–58, 75
Gypsies, 197

Hagia Sophia, 58, *59, 60*, 61, *61*, 69,
    99, *135*, 141–142, *162*, 165,
    166, 221
Hardrada, Harold, 105, 111
Harold (Anglo-Saxon king), 111
Helena (empress, wife of John VIII), 154
Helena (mother of Constantine), 18, 210
Herakleios, 67–70
Herakleios, Dynasty of, 233
Hexamilion, 152, 154
Hippodrome, 20, 21, *21*, 52, 221
History of the Church, 14
Honorius, 40, 41, 42
Hosios Loukas Monastery, 97, *97*
Hungarians/Hungary, 126, 143, 146, 152
Huns, 37, 42, 43, 45, 61–62
Hypatius, 58

icon frames (11th century), 82, *82*
icons/iconoclastic conflict, 78–79, 81,
    83–84, 86, 87, 190
immigration, 108
Irene, 83–85
Isaac II Angelos, 123, 125, 127–128
Isaurian Dynasty, 234
Isaurians, 46–47, 52
Istanbul, 219, 221–222
Isthmus of Corinth, 152, 154
Italy, 42, 45, 47, 49, 62, 63–64, 103,
    111, 112, 134, 140, 166
ivory plaque with Nativity, 83
ivory rosette casket (10th or 11th
    century), 102, *102*
Iznik, 222

Jerash, 216–217
Jerusalem, 67, 69, 210, *211*, 212
Jews, 115
John II Komnenos, 117
John V Palaiologos, 141, 143, 145
John VIII, 148, 150, 152, 154
John of Enchaita, 33
John of Phoberou, 30, 32
Julian, 24, 25–26
Justin, 53, 54
Justin II, 64–66
Justinian, 53–54, *55,* 57–58, 61–62,
    63–64, 73
Justinian, Dynasty of, 232–233
Justinian II, 75–76
Jutes, 47
Juthungi, 3

Kastoriá, 207
Khazars, 75
Kiev, 97, 99
Komneni, Dynasty of the, 236
Krum (Bulgar khan), 85–86
Kydones, Demetrius, 147

Lake Van, 222
land reforms and distribution, 67–68,
    94, 98, 101, 109, 175
languages, 9, 87–88
Laskarid Dynasty, 132, 237
Latin rule, 131–132, 134
Latins, 118–119, 128
lectionary, leaf from (post-Byzantine),
    168, *168*
Leo, 46, 47
Leo, Dynasty of, 232
Leo III, 77, 78–79, 81
Leo IV, 83
Leo V, 85–86
Leo VI, 90, 93
Leontios, 73
Lesvos Island, 204

Licinius, 13, 15, 16
lifestyle
    businessmen and trade, 182–184,
        186, 189
    clothing, *173,* 176, 179, *191,* 199, *199*
    country villages, 175–178
    farmers, 175–178
    food and diet, 176, 182–183
    imperial family, 171–172
    marriage, 179–181
    military, 198, *199,* 200–201
    Orthodox clergy, 189–190,
        192–193, 196
    outsiders, 196–198
    poor/peasantry, 172–175
    taxes and tax collectors, 177–178
    women, 178–182
livestock, 176
Lombards, 65, 83, 109, 111
Louis VII (king of France), 118
Lupicina, 53

Macedonian Dynasty, 234–235
Madaba, 217
maenad, carved bone (4th-5th
    century), 7
Manuel, 118–119, 122
Manuel II, 145, 146–148
manuscript, Psalter and New
    Testament, *113*
Manzikert (battle), 108, 109
maps
    Byzantine Empire, A.D. 565, *48*
    Byzantine Empire, A.D. 1265, *130*
    Byzantine Empire, A.D. 1355, *144*
    Constantinople, *22, 44*
    siege of Constantinople, *160*
marble chancel screen (4th-5th
    century), 40, *40*
marble relief of Mithras, 8, *8*
Marcian, 45
Mardin, 222

Marie of Antioch, 122
marriage belt (6th-7th century),
    180, *180*
Maurice, 66
Mausoleum of Galla Placidia, 213
Mausoleum of Theodoric, 213
Maxentius, 13, 14–15
Maximian, 12, 13
Maximinus Daia, 12, 13–14, 15
Mehmed, Sultan, 155, 156, 157, 159,
    161–162, 164, 165–166
Menas, Saint, 191
Mesopotamia, 66, 70–71, 108, 998
Metochites, Theodore, 138
Michael, 104
Michael I, 85
Michael II, 86
Michael III, 87
Michael V Kalaphates, 104–105
Michael VIII Palaiologos, 134, 137
military
    under Alexios Komnenos, 116
    army during 15th century, 153–154
    early Roman army life, 4–5
    infantry, mounted/cavalry, 101
    influence on emperors, 41
    lifestyle, 198, *199*, 200–201
    siege of Constantinople, 156–159,
        160, 161–165
    and the theme system, 67–68, 94
    Time of Troubles, 106
Mistra, 154, *155*, 207
monasteries
    authority and influence, 137, 193
    Benedictine, 30, 32
    Chora, 138, *138*
    Dhafní, 204, *205*
    in Egypt, 27
    Hosios Loukas, 97, *97*
    Mar-Saba in Israel, 32
    Monastery of Constantine Lips, *136*

monks, 174
Mor Gabriel (Qartmin
    Monastery), 222
Mount Athos, 140, 145, 147, 153,
    207–208
    and the Ottomans, 140
    Saffron Monastery
        (Deir-Al-Zafaran), 222
    St. John, 204
    St. Luke Stíris, 209
    Sumela in Trebizond (Trabzon), 31,
        31, 223
Moravians, 87–88
Morea, 152, 154, 161, 165
mosaics. *See also* Byzantine monuments
    Antioch, classical, *10*
    of Christ and an emperor, 91, *91*
    Christ Pantokrator (12th century),
        120, *120*
    Constantine IX and Zoe, 107, *107*
    dome, baptism of Christ, *205*
    dome, Nativity, *205*
    emperor Alexander, *92*
    loaves and fishes, 4th century,
        Tabgha, *28*
    naturalistic floor, Ein Gedi, *28, 29*
    Theodore Metochites before Christ,
        139, *139*
    Virgin and Child, apse, 89, *89*
Mosque of Omar, 70
mosques, 70, 219, 221
Mount Athos, 140, 145, 147, 153,
    207–208
Mount Nebo, 217
Muhammad, 68, 69
Murad, Sultan, 152, 155
Murano, 212
museums, 203, 204, 207, 209,
    210, 221
Muslims/Muslim armies, 69–71,
    77–78, 78, 86, 94, 96, 101,
    115, 117, 118, 123

Narses, 64
navies
  Byzantine, 68, 126, 140, 141, 143,
    147, 201
  Islamic, 70, 77
  Italian, 147
  Venetian, 117, 125, 126, 127, 132,
    134, 157, 159
Néa Ankhíalos, 208
Nestorians, doctrine of the, 45, 46
Nicaea, 131, 132, 141, 222
Nikephoros, 85
Nikephoros Phokas, 94, 96–98
Normans, 109, 111–112, 123
North Africa, 47, 61–62, 70
nosmismus (solidus), 183–184, 184
nuns and nunneries, 181

Odoacer, 47, 49
oil lamps, bronze (5th-6th century),
    177, 177, 188, 188
Omar (Arab general), 69
Omurtag (Bulgar khan), 86
Orhan (heir to Ottoman throne), 156
Osios Loukás (Hosios Loukás), 209
Ostrogoths, 37, 49–50, 62, 63–64
Ottomans, 140, 141, 142, 145–147,
    152, 156–159, 160, 161–165
outsiders in society, 196–198

Pachomius, 27
Padua, 212
paintings
  archangel Gabriel, 121
  Christ Pantokrator (17th century),
    167, 167
  Gospels of Luke and John (12th
    century), 206
  John the Baptist (16th century),
    169, 169
  murals at Vatopedhi Church (14th
    century), 208

Saint Neophytos, 124, 124
Virgin and Child (15th century),
    149, 149, 151, 151
Palace of the Despots, 207
Palaiologan Renaissance, 148
Palaiologoi, Dynasty of the, 134,
    237–238
Palaiologos, Theodore, 147
Palestine, 69
Panagia ton Chalkeon, 110
Panayía Akheiropoíetos, 209
paten, 195, 195
Patmos Island, 204
Persia/Persians, 3, 4, 24, 26, 62–63,
    64–65, 66, 67–69, 68, 70, 108,
    146–147
Peter the Hermit, 115
Philadelphia, 145
Phokas, 66–67
Phrygian Dynasty, 234
Piazza Armerina, 213
pilgrim flask (ampulla), 191
Plato, 147–148
Plethon, George Gemistus, 148
political parties, 52, 57–58, 73, 75
Procopius (court historian), 53–54, 57
Psellus, Michael, 105, 106, 190
Pulcheria, 43, 45
pyxis, ivory (15th century), 142, 142

Qal'at Si'man, 217, 218

Ravenna, 213
Raymond (prince of Antioch), 122
rebellions, 142–143, 174–175
reforms
  Basil II's, 101
  Justinian's, 54–55
  Nikephoros Phokas', 98
  theme system, 67–78, 94, 109
  Theodora's, 57

religion. *See also* churches and
   cathedrals; monasteries
Arianism, 17, 23, 39
Catholicism, 87–88
Christianity, 5–6, 9, 14–18, 25–27,
   30, 32–33, 36, 39
Christianity, schism of East and
   West, 50, 52, 83, 119, 122
conflict of the nature of Christ,
   45–46, 50, 70, 72–73, 150
Coptic Church, 33
Council of Ferrara-Florence, 147
and economy, 9
in Egypt, 27, 33
Greek Orthodox views on other
   faiths, 119
Greek Orthodoxy, 39, 87–88, 166
Hermeticism, 6, 9
Islam, 68, 69, 78, 90, 108, 143,
   196
Judaism, 196
lifestyle, Orthodox clergy,
   189–190, 192–193, 196
Mithraism, 6, 8, 9, 25–26, 27
monophytism, 50
mysticism, 193, 196
and outsiders, 196–197
Paganism, 6, 7, 8, 9, 25–27,
   32–33, 36, 39
rule of St. Benedict, 27, 30
stylites, 33
and unifying the empire, 9, 15
Union of Florence, 150, 152
Union of Lyons, 134, 137
Zoroastrianism, 64–65
religious. *See also* Crusades and
   Crusaders
authority and influence, 24–25, 39
diversity, 5–6, 9
persecutions, 6, 15–16, 16, 24, 39,
   115, 137
tax by Arabs, 69, 71

religious artifacts and relics
Christ's baby clothes, 58
crown of thorns, 132
icons/iconoclastic conflict, 78–79,
   81, 83–84, 86, 87, 190
Last Supper table, 58
Noah's hatchet, 20
True Cross, 18, 20, 58, 67, 69, 210
reliquary crosses, *95*, 133, *133*
Renaissance, 147–148, 166, 170
Rendína, 209
revolts, 142–143, 174–175
rock-cut dwellings, 220, *220*
Romanos II, 94, 96, 209
Romanos III Argyros, 104, 190
Romanos IV, 108
Rome, 18, 63–64, 215
Romulus Augustulus, 47
Rufinus, 40–41
Rumeli Hisar castle, 156
Rum Kalesi, 223
Russia, 97, 99, 166, *168*, 183

Sabas, Saint, 36
Saladin (Saracen general), 123
Sámos Island, 207
Samuel (Bulgar tsar), 98, 103
San Apollinare in Classe, 213
San Giovanni Evangelista, 213
San Miniato al Monte, 212
Santa Maria e Donato, 212
Santa Sabina, 215
Sassanids, 3, 4, 26, 62–63
Saxons, 47
sculpture, Coptic (4th century), *34*
Secret History, 53–54
Seljuk Turks, 106, 108, 109
Serbian empire, 145, 152
Severus, 12, 13
Shapur (Persian emperor), 4
signet ring, gold (6th-7th century), *187*
Silk Route, 18, 182–183

silver armband (6th-7th century), 79, *79*
Simeon, Saint, 33, 36, 217
Simeon the Great (Bulgar tsar), 98–99
Sion Treasure book covers (6th century), 194, *194*
slaves, 197–198
Slavs, 67, 68, 72, 197
society. *See* lifestyle
Sofia, 145
solidus (nosmismus), 183–184, *184*
Spain, 42, 47
Stavrakios, 85
Stilicho, 40–42
stylites, 33
Syria/Syrians, 33, 45–46, 65, 69, 98, 101

Tamerlane (Tatar general), 146
tapestries, 80, *80*
Tatars, 146–147
taxes, 116, 175, 177–178. *See also* economy
Temple Mount, 69–70
tetrarchy, 12, 229–231
Thecla, Saint, 113, *113*
Theodora (empress, wife of Justinian), 53–54, *55*, 58, 63
Theodora (empress, wife of Theophilos), 87
Theodoric (Ostrogoth king), 49–50
Theodosian Walls, 42, 43, *43*, 71, 72, 75–76, 77, 78, 222
Theodosios the Reluctant, 77
Theodosius, 39–40
Theodosius, Dynasty of, 232
Theodosius II, 42, 43, 45
Theophano (empress), 96, 98
Theophilos, 86–87
Thessaloniki, 123, 132, 140–141, 142, 143, 145, 147, 209–210
Thrace, 140, 141, 143

Tiberius Constantine, 66
timeline, 225–228
Time of Troubles, 106, 112
Torcello, 216
trade
    and cultural influence, 79, 81
    Genoese, 142, 158, 166
    and the Golden Horn, 18
    Italian, 103, 134, 140
    lifestyle, business and, 182–184, 186, 189
    Silk Route, 18, 182–183
    and Venetian merchants, 116–117
    Viking/Rus, 97
Trebizond, 131, 165, 223
True Cross, 18, 20, 58, 67, 69, 210
Turks, 64, 67, 106, 108, 109, 112, 115. *See also* Ottomans
Turnovo, 145
typhoid epidemic, 112
Tzimiskes, John, 98

Ummayad Mosque, 219
Union of Florence, 150, 152, 157
Union of Lyons, 134, 137
uprisings, 142–143, 174–175
Urban (Hungarian engineer), 158
Urban II, Pope, 112

Valens, 37–39
Valentinian II, 39
Valerian, 4
Vandals, 61
Varangian Guard, 99, 105, 111
Venetian merchants, 116–117, 142, 157
Venetians, 125–128
Venice, 103, 112, 216
Victory (pagan goddess, 4th-5th century), 7
Vikings, 97, 98, 99, 105
Villa Imperiale, 213

Villehardouin, Geoffroy de, 126–127
Visigoths, 37–39, 41, 47
Vladimir of Kiev, 99

Western empire, fall of the, 47
wheelcross (5th-6th century), *46*
William the Conqueror, 111
women's role in society, 178–182

Zákynthos, 210
Zara, 126
Zealots, 142–143, 174–175
Zeno, 46, 47, 49–50
Zeugma, 223
Zoe (empress), 94, 104, 105, 106, 190
Zosimus (pagan historian), 20, 40–41

Illustrated Histories from Hippocrene Books

Each of these volumes depicts the entire history of a region or people, from earliest times to the present. Fifty handsome black-and-white illustrations, maps, and photographs complement each book. Written in an accessible, engaging style, they are ideal for students, inquisitive travelers, and anyone interested in the heritage of a particular nation or people!

CITIES

Cracow: An Illustrated History
Zdisław Żygulski, Jr.
160 pages • 5 x 7 • 60 b/w photos/illus./maps • ISBN 0-7818-0837-5 • W • $12.95pb • (154)

London: An Illustrated History
Robert Chester & Nicholas Awde
224 pages • 5 x 7 • 360 b/w photos/illus./maps • ISBN 0-7818-0908-8 • W • $12.95pb • (300)

Moscow: An Illustrated History
Kathleen Berton Murrell
250 pages • 5 x 7 • 50 b/w photos/illus./maps • ISBN 0-7818-0945-2 • W • $14.95pb • (419)

Paris: An Illustrated History
Elaine Mokhtefi
182 pages • 5 x 7 • 50 b/w photos/illus./maps • ISBN 0-7818-0838-3 • W • $12.95pb • (136)

CIVILIZATIONS

The Arab World: An Illustrated History
Kirk Sowell
200 pages • 5½ x 8½ • 50 b/w photos/illus./maps • ISBN 0-7818-0990-8 • W • $14.95pb • (465)

The Celtic World: An Illustrated History
Patrick Lavin
185 pages • 5 x 7 • 50 b/w photos/illus./maps • ISBN 0-7818-0731-X • W • $14.95hc • (582)
185 pages • 5 x 7 • 50 b/w photos/illus./maps • ISBN 0-7818-1005-1 • W • $12.95pb • (478)

COUNTRIES

China: An Illustrated History
Yong Ho
142 pages • 5 x 7 • 50 b/w photos/illus./maps • ISBN 0-7818-0821-9 • W • $14.95hc • (542)

Egypt: An Illustrated History
Fred James Hill
160 pages • 5 x 7 • 65 b/w photos/illus./maps • ISBN 0-7818-0911-8 • W • $12.95pb • (311)

England: An Illustrated History
Henry Weisser
166 pages • 5 x 7 • 50 b/w photos/illus./maps • ISBN 0-7818-0751-4 • W • $11.95hc • (446)

France: An Illustrated History
Lisa Neal
150 pages • 5 x 7 • 50 b/w photos/illus./maps • ISBN 0-7818-0835-9 • W • $14.95hc • (105)
150 pages • 5 x 7 • 50 b/w photos/illus./maps • ISBN 0-7818-0872-3 • W • $12.95pb • (340)

Greece: An Illustrated History
Tom Stone
180 pages • 5 x 7 • 50 b/w photos/illus./maps • ISBN 0-7818-0755-7 • W • $14.95hc • (557)

India: An Illustrated History
Prem Kishore & Anuradha Kishore Ganpati
224 pages • 5 x 7 • 50 b/w photos/illus./maps • ISBN 0-7818-0944-4 • W • $14.95pb • (424)

Ireland: An Illustrated History
Henry Weisser
166 pages • 5 x 7 • 50 b/w photos/illus./maps • ISBN 0-7818-0693-3 • W • $11.95hc • (782)

Israel: An Illustrated History
David C. Gross
160 pages • 5 x 7 • 50 b/w photos/illus./maps • ISBN 0-7818-0756-5 • W • $11.95hc • (24)

Italy: An Illustrated History
Joseph F. Privitera
142 pages • 5 x 7 • 50 b/w photos/illus./maps • ISBN 0-7818-0819-7 • W • $14.95hc • (436)
Japan: An Illustrated History
Shelton Woods
200 pages • 5 x 7 • 50 b/w photos/illus./maps • ISBN 0-7818-0989-4 • W • $14.95pb • (469)
Korea: An Illustrated History from Ancient Times to 1945
David Rees
154 pages • 5 x 7 • 50 b/w photos/illus./maps • ISBN 0-7818-0873-1 • W • $12.95pb • (354)
Mexico: An Illustrated History
Michael Burke
180 pages • 5 x 7 • 50 b/w photos/illus./maps • ISBN 0-7818-0690-9 • W • $11.95hc • (585)
Poland: An Illustrated History
Iwo Cyprian Pogonowski
272 pages • 5 x 7 • 50 b/w photos/illus./maps • ISBN 0-7818-0757-3 • W • $16.95hc • (404)
Poland in World War II: An Illustrated Military History
Andrew Hempel
120 pages • 5 x 7 • 50 b/w photos/illus./maps • ISBN 0-7818-0758-1 • W • $11.95hc • (541)
120 pages • 5 x 7 • 50 b/w photos/illus./maps • ISBN 0-7818-1004-3 • W • $9.95pb • (484)
Romania: An Illustrated History
Nicolae Klepper
298 pages • 5 x 7 • 50 b/w photos/illus./maps • ISBN 0-7818-0935-5 • W • $14.95pb • (366)
Russia: An Illustrated History
Joel Carmichael
252 pages • 5 x 7 • 50 b/w photos/illus./maps • ISBN 0-7818-0689-5 • W • $14.95hc • (781)
Sicily: An Illustrated History
Joseph F. Privitera
152 pages • 5 x 7 • 50 b/w photos/illus./maps • ISBN 0-7818-0909-6 • W • $12.95pb • (301)
Spain: An Illustrated History
Fred James Hill
176 pages • 5 x 7 • 50 b/w photos/illus./maps • ISBN 0-7818-0874-X • W • $12.95pb • (339)
Tikal: An Illustrated History of the Ancient Maya Capital
John Montgomery
274 pages • 6 x 9 • 50 b/w photos/illus./maps • ISBN 0-7818-0853-7 • W • $14.95pb • (101)
Vietnam: An Illustrated History
Shelton Woods
172 pages • 5 x 7 • 50 b/w photos/illus./maps • ISBN 0-7818-0910-X • W • $14.95pb • (302)
Wales: An Illustrated History
Henry Weisser
228 pages • 5 x 7 • 50 b/w photos/illus./maps • ISBN 0-7818-0936-3 • W • $12.95pb • (418)

Also available from Hippocrene Books

A History of the Islamic World
Fred James Hill & Nicholas Awde

". . . A useful introduction to a complex and largely foreign subject . . . each chapter eschews controversy for consensus, maintaining an even-handedness that quickly earns the reader's trust."   —*Publisher's Weekly*

224 pages • 5½ x 8½ • 65 b/w photos/illus./maps • ISBN 0-7818-1015-9 • $22.50hc • (545)

All prices are subject to change without prior notice. To order **Hippocrene Books**, contact your local bookstore, call (718) 454-2366, visit www.hippocrenebooks.com, or write to: Hippocrene Books, 171 Madison Avenue, New York, NY 10016. Please enclose check or money order adding $5.00 shipping (UPS) for the first book and $.50 for each additional title.